Glen Hancock

Home budgeting

Oyez Publishing Limited London and Ward Lock Limited

First published in Great Britain in 1979 jointly
by Ward Lock Limited, 116 Baker Street,
London W1M 2BB, a member of the Pentos Group and Oyez Publishing
Limited, Norwich House, 11/13 Norwich Street, London EC4A 1AB.

Designed by Grant Gibson

Text filmset in Plantin
Printed and bound in Great Britain by
Cox & Wyman Ltd, London, Fakenham and Reading

British Library Cataloguing in Publication Data
Hancock, Glen
Home budgeting.
1. Home economics – Accounting
I. Title
640'.42 TX326

ISBN 0-7063-5517-2
0-7063-5696-9 Pbk

Contents

Caution

Changes in the cost of living brought about by inflation and the Chancellor of the Exchequer's Budget are just two of many good reasons for having a sensible budget for the family. However, it also means that any costs quoted in the book can be subjected to changes for the same reasons, and to varying degrees at short notice. Readers are therefore advised to ascertain for themselves the up-to-date costs of any item quoted in this book.

Preface

The author could be accused of having his hypothetical family too well organised with his family budget – so much so that in trying to make it work he produces a rigidly programmed life style without any flexibility to allow the family to do whatever they want to do with their time and money. This is not so! Having a family budget is simply a means of ensuring that you do not spend more money than you earn.

There are certain payments in your budget which have to be made. After you have accounted for those payments you can spend the rest of your money on whatever you like – but not without having control, and the only way of monitoring your income and expenditure is to do your sums properly and as simply as you can.

It is hoped that reading this book will help you to do that, but at the same time the author acknowledges that because of the many permutations of different circumstances which exist in all families, it is a quite impossible task to write an easily read book which comprehensively covers all aspects of preparing and keeping to a budget for the family. In terms of money only one thing is common to all families – all receive income and all have expenses of one sort or another. Whatever the family's income is, a certain proportion of it is spent on items which are common to most families, eg rent, rates, gas, insurances and so on. These are fairly predictable items of expenditure and will not normally spring any surprises on your budget – it is the unpredictable or unexpected item of expenditure which creates financial problems.

The author has endeavoured to draw to your attention as many items of expenditure as he can, in the hope that you will not overlook any of your income or expenditure when preparing your family budget. Regrettably, he cannot tell you how much or how little all of those expenses ought to be, but he does offer some guidance in the following pages.

Chapter 1

Introduction – a guide to family budgeting

The object of any form of family budget is to try to ensure that the family does not spend more than it can comfortably afford to, out of the income it receives. The word 'family' is used rather than 'husband' or 'wife' or both, because most members of any family generate some form of income, be it in the form of a pension, government grant, Child Benefits (Family Allowance), or a wage earned. Likewise, all members of the family spend money, or have money spent on them, therefore their collective earnings and expenditure have an effect on the household finances.

Some families are fortunate enough to have sufficient income not to worry too much about detailed control of their money, but there must be millions of families who are not so fortunate, particularly in times of high unemployment and wage control.

Even those families who have a regular and adequate income cannot afford to be complacent about their financial status, with the ever present threat of redundancy in so many industries, rising prices of commodities, and increased rents and rates. It is therefore becoming more and more important that every family should take stock of what it earns and how much it spends, so that they can be sure that whenever they spend money on furniture, holidays, gifts, or have to find money for some unexpected event (such as a speeding fine, television repair, motor or household accident) they can account for it out of their income and adjust either their spending or earnings accordingly.

Inability to control their money must be an increasing cause for concern among many families. Lack of control often leads to difficulties, anxiety and even illness.

How many families or individuals work out a budget for themselves, but give up after a short while because they cannot work to it, or keep proper control over it? They become uninterested, even frightened, of comparing what they spend and what they earn. They can only carry on as they always have done in the past, hoping that 'everything will turn out all right in the end'. This kind of hope is becoming more and more impossible to realise, because just as wage control and high unemployment inhibit the generation of more income, rising prices prevent any drastic cuts in family expenditure.

The probable reason for a family not being able to live within a budget which they have set for themselves, is not that they had no idea of their collective income, but because either they did not appreciate the full extent of their outgoing payments, or, if they did, had not allowed sufficient money for some or all of the items in their budget.

There can, of course, be exceptional circumstances which make it difficult to keep to your budget, and these are dealt with in Chapter 5.

While it is not possible to list every item of expenditure which a family could expect to meet, it is hoped that reading this book will provide those preparing a family budget with a better idea of what to include, how to calculate future expenditure, and how to set it out on paper in a simple but effective manner. It is also hoped that it will equip you with the necessary foresight to anticipate how your budget will change when the pattern of your life changes – such as when you buy a new home, when you start a family, when the children start school, when they get married and so on.

There are many statistics available giving the national average wage earned, and what the public spends on a variety of commodities per average person, but if you are not an average wage earner or an average spender these statistics are of little use to you. Your budget is very personal to your family and although statistics can be a good guide, only you can decide how you wish to divide your income to meet your expenses.

Whilst it is relatively simple to make an approximate total of your average weekly expenses, this gives no indication of how much cash you have available at any particular time of the year to spend on say, a holiday, or a new television set, or to pay an unexpected tax demand. The type of budget sheet which provides this information is shown in *Figure 1*. You do not need to be an accountant or even particularly clever to be able to operate this type of budget, but you do need to have a good idea of how much you have spent in the past on such items as electricity, gas, telephone, rent, rates, etc.

There are three parts to the family budget shown in *Figure 1*.

SECTION 1	INCOME	*see* Chapter 2
SECTION 2	EXPENDITURE	*see* Chapter 3
SECTION 3	CONTROL OVER INCOME AND EXPENDITURE	*see* Chapter 4

You will see that there are two spaces against each line in each section. The top space is used to write in the figures which you forecast what you will earn or spend in each month of the year, or whatever period you decide to budget for. The bottom line is used to write in the amounts which you *actually* earn or spend each month over the same period. If the two figures are entered in different coloured inks, the comparison of the figures will be made so much easier. (In this book different coloured inks are represented by shading some columns.)

Having made your budget or forecast of what you think you will earn and spend, it is very important to enter the amounts which you *actually* earn and spend, not only how much but also when you *actually* earned and spent the money. Even though the amounts and dates may be completely different to your forecast, this will make the job of drawing up your budget for the next period a simpler task because in addition to having a better idea of how much you spent on any particular item, you will also have a better idea of when you will require the money to meet that cost in your next budget.

Before giving an explanation of each item on the budget sheet, here are a few useful tips worth remembering:

1 Whenever you have made a budget or forecast NEVER alter any of the figures, regardless of how inaccurate they may subsequently turn out

Section		Income [1979]	Jan	Feb	Mar	Apr	May	Jun	Jul	Aug	Sep	Oct	Nov	Dec	Total
	1	Husband													
	2	Wife													
	3	Child benefits													
	4	Other													
	5														
Section 1	6	Total income													
		Expenditure													
	7	Husband													
	8	Wife													
	9	Mortgage													
	10	Ground rent and rates													
	11	Electricity													
	12	Gas													
	13	Telephone													
	14	Heating													
	15	Insurance													
	16	Television													
	17	Clothes													
	18	Car													
	19	Anniversaries													
	20	Christmas and holidays													
	21	House and garden maintenance													
	22	Furnishings													
	23	Sports club													
	24	Childrens' sports/hobbies													
	25	Freezer stocks													
	26	Sundries													
Section 2	27	Total expenditure													
	28														
	29														
	30														
Section 3	31														

Figure 1

to be. If your budget starts to go wildly incorrect the best thing to do is to draw up another budget commencing from the date it goes uncontrollably wrong. The reason for not altering figures is that you can look back at your budget, see where you went wrong and what to do in subsequent budgets to correct it. If you start altering figures you will very likely make a mess of the final arithmetic of your budget and you will lose interest in it.

2 Electronic calculators for simple additions can be obtained at reasonable prices and save a lot of time and effort.

3 Wherever possible you should pay everything by cheque. The counterfoils in your cheque book provide one of the best records of your expenditure and you will find that you can total your monthly expenditure much more easily. If you pay cash out of your pocket you may find it very difficult to account for how you have spent it – even if you have a good memory!

4 There are four months in every year with an extra week making them a 'five week month'. If you are paid weekly you should make an increased allowance in both your income and expenditure in these 'five week months'. If you are paid monthly the 'five week months' will not usually affect your income, but they will affect your expenditure and it should be allowed for accordingly. It is fairly common practice with the use of payroll computers, for salaried people to be paid every four weeks instead of monthly, which means thirteen pay days per annum instead of twelve. In this instance, you would still forecast and record the receipt of your income in the months in which you are actually paid, except that one month you would have two pay days.

5 If you have not previously prepared a family budget, you will have to be persistent in preparing your first one, not because it is difficult, but because you will need to spend some time researching your past expenditure, to see how much you have spent on certain items and when you had to pay for them. Seventy-five per cent of the accuracy

with which you prepare your budget depends on what historical cost information is available about your previous expenditure. Also, if you are buying anything in your budget by way of hire-purchase instalments, you will need to establish, before preparing your budget, how many payments are outstanding on each item. However, once you have done this exercise and you have worked through your first twelve months' budget, you will find that the subsequent budgets are very easily prepared in a matter of one or two hours, including the tedious task of adding up all of the columns and lines across.

6 There is no reason why the preparation of your budget should not involve all members of the family, including the children if they are old enough to understand, not necessarily the arithmetic, but the aims and objects of having a budget for the family to work to. For example, open family discussions about their requirements for clothing, equipment for sport and hobbies, anniversary gifts, school outings, furnishings, etc, will perhaps ensure that your forecasting in respect of this expenditure is more accurate. Likewise, if you have determined in your budget the amount of money you can spend on a holiday, the family could then discuss and decide the type of holiday they would like and can afford out of the money available. If you do this you may well find that the family, especially the children, will understand more readily the reasons for not being able to have many of the things they would like to have, and why, if they have one thing, then they have to go without something else. Children will learn from this, and if it educates them in handling money and prepares them for the time when they have to prepare and control their own budgets, then open discussions such as this can only do good. However, in order to do this it is necessary for every member of the family to be open and honest about their income and expenses. To some members of the family the idea of disclosing such information may be totally unacceptable. This will obviously make the family budget difficult to compile and operate, but if your family is in financial difficulties, a change of attitude may be necessary in the interests of keeping your financial head above water.

7 Finally, your attention is drawn to the words of caution at the front of this book. It is unavoidable that certain present-day costs must be quoted at the time of printing, and that sooner rather than later these costs will be out of date. You are therefore again advised to check the up-to-date costs of any item quoted in this book before using the information yourself, but remember that this book is more about giving guidance as to how to prepare a budget using you own figures (which should be up-to-date) rather than telling you how much you should be spending or what to spend your money on.

Chapter 2

Section 1:

Income

Figure 2

Lines 1 and 2 – Husband and wife's income

Section 1	Income [1979]	Jan	Feb	Mar	Apr	May	Jun	Jul	Aug	Sep	Oct	Nov	Dec	Total
1	Husband	395	395	395	395	395	395	395	395	395	395	395	395	4740
2	Wife	60	60	60	75	60	60	75	60	75	60	60	75	780
3	Child benefits	48	48	48	60	48	48	60	48	60	48	48	60	624
4	Other				10						10			20
5														
6	Total income	503	503	503	540	503	503	530	503	530	513	503	530	6164

Enter in the top of Lines 1 and 2 the amount which the husband and wife earn each month, as shown above. Do not forget those 'five week months', in this example they are April, July, September, and December. Enter only the amount you actually receive after all deductions have been made for tax, insurance, etc. This is easily done if you are a regular wage earner receiving a regular amount each week or month. It is not so easy if, for instance, you have to rely on making a sales commission or working overtime to make up your income, especially if your commission or overtime fluctuates from month to month. If this is the case you may have to take a view of what you think you can earn as compared with what you forecast in SECTION 2: EXPENDITURE, as being the minimum amount you must earn to meet your spending, as discussed later on page 84. Never be over ambitious in forecasting your earnings. It is better NOT to anticipate wage increases or bonuses. If you enter the ordinary amount you receive in January for each month of the year, any subsequent increases or bonuses you receive can be a useful reserve. If you do *not* receive pay for certain holidays you must remember to adjust your income in the months when those holidays are taken.

Line 3 – Child Benefits (formerly known as Family Allowance)

3	Child benefits	48	48	48	60	48	48	60	48	60	48	48	60	624

There are many and varied types of grants, pensions, and supplementary benefits, available from both private and government sources. Child Benefits or Family Allowance, has been shown in this example rather than any one of the many other allowances because it is typical for many families. If you receive an allowance of any description enter the amount on this line. You can of course include any additional regular allowances which you receive under the heading or on another spare line. In this example the three children are eligible for family allowance at the rate of £4·00 each per week.

Line 4 – Other income

4	Other				10						10			20

This line is intended to cover forecasted incidental income and also the receipt of unexpected income. It could be a multitude of things such as bank interest, dividends from shares, a win on the premium bonds or football pools, an inheritance, or just a gift of money. It could also be a profit from the sale of property, car, antiques, furniture, or a government grant for the improvement of your home. In this example, dividend from shares amounting to £10.00 is shown as being receivable in April and October.

Line 5

5														

If you have any further sources of income such as a working son or daughter, or alternatively if you receive an allowance from your employer for running your own car in your job, you may need this spare line.

Line 6 – Total

6	Total income	503	503	503	540	503	503	530	503	530	513	503	530	6164

Total your income for each month on this line and in the final column the addition of each month's income will give you a total of your income for the year. Also in the final column is the total received from each source of income from Lines 1 to 5. Check that your additions are correct both vertically and horizontally.

Chapter 3

Section 2:

Expenditure

Remember that the easiest way of keeping a record of your spending is to pay for as many purchases as you can by cheque, and also by making helpful notes on the counterfoils of your cheque book. If there is more than one person paying out cheques in your family you may find it easier if you have a joint current account at your bank so that all of your incoming and outgoing payments made by cheque will appear on one 'end of the month statement' from your bank.

You will see in *Figure 3* a list of typical items of expenditure which a family of five people can expect to meet. It is a hypothetical budget intended to be used as a guide only and to help create an awareness of where your money goes. It is not intended to be indicative of the proportions into which your own budget should be divided – that is a matter for you to decide entirely.

There may be some items on this list which do not apply to your own budget and equally there may be other items which you will want to add to the list. Try to allow a separate line for each item of income and expenditure. If you have too many items grouped together, the money totals at the end of your budget period will not be helpful in forecasting succeeding budgets. There is a check list of items which may apply to your budget at the end of this book.

Remember those 'five week months'! In this example they are in April, July, September and December.

Section		Income [1979]	Jan	Feb	Mar	Apr	May	Jun	Jul	Aug	Sep	Oct	Nov	Dec	Total
Section 1	1	Husband	395	395	395	395	395	395	395	395	395	395	395	395	4740
	2	Wife	60	60	60	75	60	60	75	60	75	60	60	75	780
	3	Child benefits	48	48	48	60	48	48	60	48	60	48	48	60	624
	4	Other				10						10			20
	5														
	6	Total income	503	503	503	540	503	503	530	503	530	513	503	530	6164
Section 2		Expenditure				5 weeks			5 weeks		5 weeks			5 weeks	
	7	Husband	72	72	72	90	72	72	90	72	90	72	72	90	936
	8	Wife	120	120	120	150	120	120	150	120	150	120	120	150	1560
	9	Mortgage	50	50	50	50	50	50	50	50	50	50	50	50	600
	10	Ground rent and rates	120	15					100	35					270
	11	Electricity	30			40			20			30			120
	12	Gas			15			15			10			10	50
	13	Telephone	15			20			15			15			65
	14	Heating	35			60			30			15			140
	15	Insurance	8	8	8	20	8	8	8	8	18	8	8	8	118
	16	Television	10	10	10	31	10	10	10	10	10	10	10	10	141
	17	Clothes	20	20	20	25	20	20	25	20	25	20	20	25	260
	18	Car	25	85	25	75	30	25	25	25	25	25	25	25	415
	19	Anniversaries	10		5		10		15	15	5				60
	20	Christmas and holidays		40		20				520				100	680
	21	House and garden maintenance			25			25			25			25	100
	22	Furnishings	15	15	15	15	15	15	15	15	15	15	15	15	180
	23	Sports club			20							80			100
	24	Childrens' sports/hobbies	15				15				15				45
	25	Freezer stocks		30			30			30			30		120
	26	Sundries			25			25			25			25	100
	27	Total expenditure	543	465	410	596	380	385	553	920	463	460	350	533	6060
Section 3	28														
	29														
	30														
	31														

Figure 3 Budget for family of five (three children at school)

Lines 7 and 8 – Husband's and wife's allowance

7	Husband	72	72	72	90	72	72	90	72	90	72	72	90	936
8	Wife	120	120	120	150	120	120	150	120	150	120	120	150	1560

These two items are the most difficult items to forecast with any degree of accuracy, mainly because of the difficulty of deciding what the respective cash allowances of the husband and wife are intended to cover.

Questions as to whether the wife's allowance includes a 'wage' for being housekeeper or is it solely intended to cover food purchases and other consumable household goods, or whether the husband's allowance is purely pocket money, can only be dealt with by the individual. Everyone has their own views about these two items, but it does not really matter what arrangements you have as long as you set it out properly in your budget.

It is a good idea to make the husband's and wife's allowances cover the items for which you normally pay cash out of your pocket. Draw up a list of these items so that you do not enter duplicate payments in your forecast or in your record of actual spending.

It would be possible to go into great detail as to how to calculate the separate amounts for the husband's and wife's allowances, but more usually it is a matter of trial and error over a few weeks, commencing with a lower amount and gradually increasing, if necessary, until eventually you deduce the weekly minimum amount required to enable you to live at the standard you desire or to which you have become accustomed. If you subsequently find the cost of that standard to be such that it will not permit you to spend the amounts required to meet the expenses of the other essential items in your budget, you may have to trim down the husband's and wife's allowances accordingly. In the *Figure 3* example, the husband's and wife's allowances jointly account for over 40 per cent of the income received, and it is obvious therefore, that if economies were necessary to keep this budget on course, these two allowances would have to be closely scrutinised. More about this in Chapters 5 and 7.

In this budget the amount shown against the husband's and wife's allowances is intended to cover the following items:

Husband	*Wife*
Smoking	All food (excluding large purchases of meat for freezer)
Entertaining	Toiletries, kitchen and other consumable household goods
Drinking	School meals and bus fares
Eating out	Hairdressing and cosmetics
Newspapers	
Children's pocket money	
Theatre/cinema	

If the wife keeps the family allowance and all of her own wages you must remember to add these sums to the amount allowed out of the husband's wage. Otherwise you will have a distorted view of what you actually spend on food and consumable non-food items.

Line 9 – Mortgage or rent

9	Mortgage	50	50	50	50	50	50	50	50	50	50	50	50	600

This item is usually an easy sum to enter in the budget as it will be well known to you and changes in the monthly amount you pay are not very frequent over any twelve monthly period. If you pay a weekly rent watch out for those 'five week months'.

Line 10 – Ground rent/rates

10	Ground rent and rates	120	15					100	35					270

If you live in rented accommodation where the rent is inclusive of all rates, then this item will obviously not appear on your budget sheet, but if you should decide to buy your own home, or if you change your accommodation to different 'rates exclusive' terms then you will need to provide for this item in your budget. If you own leasehold property you may be paying ground rent in addition to the rates which you pay to the Local Authority. All these types of payments usually become due on set dates twice annually, but you may not be obliged to pay the amounts on those dates, so enter the amounts in the months in which you intend to pay them (as with any other similar payments in your budget). In this example the expenditure on Line 10 comprises £100.00 rates, £20.00 ground rent and £15.00 water rates, each payable twice annually.

Lines 11, 12 and 13 – Electricity, gas and telephone

11	Electricity	30			40			20			30			120
12	Gas			15			15			10			10	50
13	Telephone	15			20			15			15			65

Normally you can expect to receive four quarterly accounts for your telephone and for gas and electricity consumed in the household. Not everyone receives their bills at the same time so you will need to look at your past accounts to see when you paid them and how much they were. From this information it is fairly easy to make a forecast of what you will spend on these items in the forthcoming year, after making some allowance for increased costs, which are usually advised by the respective Authorities well in advance of any increased charges becoming effective. Remember also to make an allowance for increases in your electricity bill due to the acquisition of extra electrical appliances in the home.

Line 14 – Heating

14	Heating	35			60			30			15			140

If you have gas fired heating, then you probably will not be able to separate the cost of heating from the total amount of your gas bill: unless, of course, you use gas only for heating and not for cooking. However, if you have oil fired, solid fuel or off-peak electric heating you will be able to segregate this cost. The reason for separating this item and not grouping it under Lines 11 and 12 is that this is an item which you can economise on if it is necessary to do so, in order to keep your total expenditure within your earnings. This matter is dealt with more fully in Chapter 7. Any costs for annual insurance, maintenance or servicing of the heating plant should also be allowed for in this part of your budget.

Line 15 – Insurance

15	Insurance	8	8	8	20	8	8	8	8	18	8	8	8	118

Once you have taken out insurance protection the premium you pay usually remains constant for a long period. It is easy therefore to enter the amounts you pay simply by looking at your policy or policies to determine the amounts and due dates. The premiums may be payable once or twice a year, monthly or weekly, in which case watch out for those 'five week months'. There are many and varied types of insurance which a family could become involved in, and to describe all of the eventualities which you can insure against would take up more space than there is in the remainder of this book but what you should be looking for is the protection of those assets which make up your budget. For example, how would the family survive on their budget if the main source of income were temporarily or permanently removed? How would the wife perpetuate the budget if she lost her husband? How would she pay all bills and meet the remaining expenses on the budget, and keep the family as comfortably as they were kept previously? Surely, what you would want to do is to :

a Insure the main breadwinner against his or her death or disabling accident/illness, coupled with cash benefits on expiration of the policy.
b Provide the surviving partner with an income to carry on the business of running and working to the family budget if she or he cannot earn sufficient to do so.
c Provide the family with a roof over their heads free of any burdens.
d Provide the children with a good education.
e Protect the contents of the house. You may have put a lot of hard

earned money into furnishing and equipping your home, and it is cheaper to protect it than to have to replace it at your own expense. This type of insurance will cost in the order of 25p per £100.00 value of contents insured per annum.

Points (a) and (b) can be coupled together but there are a variety of ways in which the husband or wife can be insured, and it is advisable to consult a reputable insurance company as to which sort of insurance suits you and your income. There is nothing to prevent you from obtaining a number of alternative quotations from different insurance companies so that you can be satisfied that you are getting the best deal for yourself.

If you have a mortgage to buy your own home then usually the source from which you have borrowed the money will insist that you insure your home for the present day cost of replacing it. Remember that in times of high inflation you will need to increase the sum insured from time to time in order to keep up with increased building costs.

There are other events where special insurance protection can be provided, eg holidays, luggage, and birth of twins, but there is a limit to what you can afford to pay out of your income, and again it is up to the individual to decide the priorities of essential insurance.

Most insurance payments will be entered on Line 15 Insurance, but if you pay separate insurance for your television and car it is advisable that this cost should be entered on Lines 16 and 18, so that at the end of the year you can see the true total of how much per annum each item has cost you. In this example the insurance payments comprise a monthly payment of £8.00 for life and mortgage protection insurance, £12.00 per annum insurance of the house and £10.00 insurance for the contents of the house.

Line 16 – Television

16	Television	10	10	10	31	10	10	10	10	10	10	10	10	141

Obviously everything you pay out in respect of your television is entered on this line, whether it be the monthly rental you pay or the amount you pay for the hire-purchase of your television set. If you own your television then you may pay an annual maintenance scheme or insurance premium, but if you do not then you would be wise to make an allowance for breakdown repairs, especially as your television set gets older. Your set will not, however, last forever and at some stage in one of your budgets you must be prepared to make provision for the eventual replacement of your set. This can be done by lump sum outright purchase, hire-purchase, or with a rental set. If you have kept proper records of what owning a television set has cost you over its life, then you can compare the cost of purchase with rental over a long period and decide whether or not to purchase another set rather than rent one.

It is for this reason that all of the costs connected with your television set, including insurance, should be recorded on this line of your budget. Of course you have to renew your television licence on the same date each year so enter the appropriate amount under that month (£21.00 per annum for colour, £9.00 for black and white). The figures used in the example are based on the rent for a colour television at the rate of £10.00 per month plus the licence at £21.00, renewable in April.

Line 17 – Clothes

17	Clothes	20	20	20	25	20	20	25	20	25	20	20	25	260

The amount which the family spends on clothing is a difficult one to forecast and will vary considerably from one family to another, even families of the same size and age group, depending on whether you dress extravagantly or moderately. There is no magic formula by which you can calculate this sum, and if you have no idea at all how much your family spends on clothing, your first budget estimate will be more of a shot in the dark than a carefully calculated sum.

You could, however, attempt to arrive at an approximate cost by making a list of clothing which is essential for each member of the family for the forthcoming year. Set a price against each item and arrive at a lump sum which you think it will cost you. Divide the sum by twelve and enter the answer under each month. As you purchase clothing for the family during the year you will be able to see after six months whether your clothing budget is working to plan. If it is not, then you know that you will have to cut back your spending on clothing over the next six months' period, unless you can cut back on some other item in your budget where you have surplus money. Similarly, if you are not spending as much as you thought you would on clothing, you may be able to use this saving to offset against some other item on which you are overspending, in order to keep your overall budget in control.

Watch out for clothing required for special events such as weddings, the firm's annual dinner-dance; and even one of your children changing schools can require up to £55.00 for the very basic uniform.

After you have worked through one or two actual budgets you will have a much better idea of what clothing the family really costs you, and you will be able to forecast more accurately in subsequent budgets.

Line 18 – Car

18	Car	25	85	25	75	30	25	25	25	25	25	25	25	415

If you are provided with a car as part of your job then you will probably only be concerned with petrol purchased for your own mileage. If you own a car, or cars, and pay all of the purchase and running expenses, then you will need to make provision for the following expenses:

a *Hire-purchase payments* If you are buying your car by hire-purchase instalments, show the monthly amounts you have to pay. If you pay weekly instalments remember those 'five week months'.

b *Road tax* This will cost you £50.00 if you pay it once per annum, but if you pay it every four months this will cost you £18.35 each time, making the total annual cost £55.05.

c *Insurance* The amount you pay for insurance is influenced by many factors, and when you have determined all of these you can insert the appropriate amount under the month in which the premium payment is due. How much you pay depends on your record as a driver, the insurance group into which your type of car falls, the type of insurance required by you, where you live and what no claims discount you are entitled to. If you have not previously taken out car insurance and have no idea what it will cost you, it pays to shop around a few reputable insurance companies for alternative premium quotations.

d *Oil and petrol* Obviously the amount you spend depends on the mileage your vehicle travels over twelve months. If you know from the mileometer in your car how many miles you travelled over the previous twelve months and it is fairly typical of the mileage you normally travel, then simply divide that mileage by the number of miles per gallon that your vehicle will motor at. When you have worked out how many gallons you will need to purchase over twelve months, you can calculate the total annual cost which, when divided by twelve, will give you the monthly cost. Similarly, if you need a pint of oil every 1,000 miles you can calculate the addition to be made to your petrol costs over twelve months to cover the cost of oil. If you receive a mileage or other car allowance from your employer towards the running costs of your vehicle, then this should be shown in your budget as INCOME; unless, of course, you keep this remuneration in your pocket as spending or housekeeping money, in which case it should be entered as part of the husband's or wife's allowance as appropriate.

e *Servicing and maintenance* The number of times your vehicle requires to be serviced is again determined by dividing your mileage per annum by the frequency which the vehicle manufacturer recommends for servicing, eg every 3,000 miles. The cost of servicing depends on whether you do it yourself or take it to your garage. Your garage will tell you how much it will normally cost for your type of car to have a standard service, but usually there will be small parts to pay for in addition. If you service your car yourself you will need a set of tools and there may be certain parts of the service which have to be carried out by your garage, such as wheel alignment, timing, etc, and of course if your vehicle is over three years old it has to be subjected to annual MOT tests which will cost about £4.50 plus any repairs required as a result of the test.

f *Repairs/replacements* The amount to allow in your budget for this item is very difficult to forecast, as the cost is so variable from one car to another – even cars of the same make and age. Obviously the older your car is the greater the cost of repairs and replacements will be, but nevertheless you must make an allowance of some sort. A good guide to this can be obtained from the Consumers Association magazine *Which* (car buying guide) but this is one item which you as an individual must assess for yourself, and in doing so you will need to decide whether you are a 'hard' or a 'careful' driver, particularly in respect of such matters as tyres, brakes and gear box.

g *AA/RAC or other motorist club membership* This cost is part of the running cost of your car. The fees vary depending on the facilities available to you, but if you belong to one of these organisations you will probably pay an annual membership fee, which should be shown.

h *Car Wash Club* If you pay for this as a member of a club, again an annual fee may be due.

i *Driving licence* If you are still learning to drive you may need to provide in your budget for driving lessons at a Driving School plus your provisional driving licence, which will cost £1.50 per annum. It will cost a further £6.75 to take your driving test. When you have passed your test your driving licence will cost £5.00 and this will last you until the age of seventy.

j *Garage* If you pay a separate rent for a garage in which to keep your car then this cost should be shown in your budget as part of the running cost of your car.

Depreciation is excluded from the list because it is not a sum which you pay monthly directly out of your pocket or bank account. Loss through depreciation can be shown as a direct expense when you allow in your budget for the inevitable replacement of your vehicle. For example if you decided to change your car in August and your new car was going to cost you £3,000 less the value of your present car, say £2,000, then obviously your direct expense in the month of August is £1,000, or if you are buying on hire-purchase the direct monthly expense is the amount of each hire-purchase instalment. So although you can say that your car costs you 'x' pounds per week in depreciation, it does not affect your budget until you need to provide for it in your budget. It could be of course that you make a profit on the replacement of your vehicle, in which case you would enter the profit on Line 4 under INCOME.

Line 19 – Anniversaries

19	Anniversaries	10		5		10		15	15	5				60

If you analyse what this means you might be surprised to find that you are spending a fair amount of money every month on gifts and greetings cards either for your own family, or other families and friends, on birthdays, wedding anniversaries, Mother's Day, Father's Day, Valentine's Day, etc. Write out a list in order of priority and set a sum against each event. Group the events under the months in which the expenditure occurs but you may be surprised at the annual cost! If you have a forthcoming special anniversary to celebrate, such as a Silver Wedding or coming of age, you may have to increase this item to cover the extra cost of those special celebrations and gifts.

Line 20 – Christmas and holidays

20	Christmas and holidays		40		20				520				100	680

You may be able to dispense with a holiday but if there is one thing which is indispensable it must be Christmas, and therefore you should allocate a sum of money in December or even earlier to cover the extraordinary cost of Christmas food, cards, presents, drink, travelling and entertaining, over and above your normal expenditure. In this example you will see that a sum of £100.00 has been allowed in the month of December to cover the cost of Christmas spending.

The cost of a holiday must be one of the largest single items of non-essential expenditure in your budget and should be looked at very carefully. It is all very well booking a summer holiday at Christmas, but how many do this and really know whether they will be able to pay for it when the time comes to go away on the holiday? If your budget does nothing else for you, it will at least tell you what cash you have available for a holiday at any given time of the year. You may well find, however, that when you have allowed for all other essential items of your budget, your holiday will have to be geared to suit whatever money is left over, if any, and timed to suit a month when you have the money available. If you look at the sample budget in *Figure 4* (page 38) you will see by looking along Line 30 that the earliest month in which the holiday can be afforded is August because there is insufficient money available in the earlier months.

When assessing the overall cost of your family holiday be careful not to overlook any ancillary expenses which are *not* included either in the basic holiday cost or in your spending money – such things as passports, travelling (including to and from the airport and station), car parking, insurances; and if you have a pet dog, cat, fish or anything which has to be cared for whilst you are away on holiday, there could be kennel or similar charges to make allowance for. If you book a holiday in advance you will usually need to find a deposit of between £2.00 and £5.00 per person at the time of booking and the balance to be paid either prior to or at the time of taking your holiday. In the *Figure 3* example, a deposit of £40.00 for a holiday is paid in February with the balance plus spending money being paid in August. If the holiday was for two weeks, it could be your view that whilst your family is away from home for two weeks, the husband's and wife's allowance on Lines 7 and 8 should be reduced accordingly, because the family's absence from home means no expenditure on food, etc. In practice this does not work because you may find that as the holiday draws near you find yourself buying extra bits and pieces for the holiday, and similarly when you return there seem to be extra groceries to purchase, so for this reason the full allowances to the husband and wife have been shown during the month the holiday is taken. If, however, you take a holiday longer than two weeks then it would be reasonable to reduce the husband's and wife's allowances for that period to release more cash for your holiday budget. If you take a late or early winter holiday at 'off peak' season prices, not only will you benefit from the reduced cost, but you may also make other savings not normally made by taking a holiday in the summer months. For example, a two week winter holiday could show a saving on your heating bill of between 10 and 15 per cent. Do not forget that holidays not only mean your annual two, three or four weeks but also Bank Holidays. In *Figure 3*, £20.00 has been allowed in April for Bank Holiday expenses. Many schools include as part of their curriculum visits to foreign countries, and your children may not want to miss out on these trips abroad, which means that part of your holiday budget will need to be allocated for this event.

If you go on a touring holiday using your own car then some of the cost of running the car should be allocated to holidays rather than to the car budget. Remember to adjust your income if you are not paid for the time taken off for holidays.

Line 21 – House and garden maintenance

21	House and garden maintenance			25			25			25			25	100

Whether you own your home or not, you will be faced with expenditure of one sort or another in repairing and redecorating the accommodation in which you live – unless of course you live in accommodation where the landlord or someone else is entirely responsible for such costs. It is a false economy to disregard the proper maintenance of your home, as lack of attention to it will lead to fabric and structural deterioration requiring remedial treatment more expensive than the cost of proper maintenance, apart from depreciating the value of the property. This applies particularly to older property and to exterior decorations which should be carried out at intervals not exceeding two and a half years. It could of course require doing more frequently, depending on how well it was decorated previously or how exposed it is to the weather. The frequency with which you decorate interior accommodation is for the individual to decide. The amount which you spend on repairs and decorations again depends on the size and age of the property, and also whether you do it yourself or pay someone else to do it for you. Make a list of rooms which will require repair/redecoration and set a sum against each room including, if necessary, external repairs and redecoration. Insert the amounts under the month in which you intend to have the work carried out.

If you are laying out your garden for the first time you will require cash for shrubs, plants, paving and walling materials, tools, equipment and garden furniture. You may need to spread the development of your garden over a few years, depending on how ambitious your intended layout is, in order to keep the cost within your budget. Once your garden is established and you have acquired sufficient tools to keep the garden well tended, your budget need only make allowance for the provision of new plants, shrubs, fertiliser and any special projects you have planned for your garden. If you have a lot of mechanical garden equipment there will be maintenance and repairs to cater for in your budget.

Line 22 – Furnishings

22	Furnishings	15	15	15	15	15	15	15	15	15	15	15	15	180

Anything which you buy for the house (other than decorating or gardening materials) is classified as furnishings. If you are still in the process of setting up your first home you will obviously be anxious to furnish it in the style you want as quickly as possible, and therefore a large proportion of your budget will be devoted to this item. List the furniture you require in the order of priority, set the price you want to pay, or the price you have to pay for what you want, against each item. If you need guidance as to what you need you may find Mary Gilliat's book *Setting Up Home* (published by Arrow Books Limited) interesting reading. Decide how you intend to purchase the furniture – by instalments or cash – and work into your budget what you can afford to pay out of it. Once you have established your home you will spend less and less on furnishing but nevertheless there is still always room for additional and replacement furniture. As your family grows up and their furniture requirements change from cots to beds, or chests of drawers to wardrobes, you will need to anticipate these changes within your budget.

As with your television, it is possible to have a maintenance agreement or insurance protection for mechanical equipment in the home such as refrigerators, cookers, washers, dryers, vacuum cleaners and stereo equipment, as they are all capable of breakdown and will require periodic maintenance and repair. Eventually certain items, if not all, will require replacement when they reach the stage of being incapable of economic repair, but as the life span of most of this type of furniture is relatively long, it is not an item which will appear very frequently in your budget. Nevertheless preventative maintenance will lengthen the life of some of your mechanical equipment, particularly washing machines and dryers, and you may consider it prudent to pay an annual maintenance or insurance premium.

Line 23 – Sports club

23	Sports club			20							80			100

'Sports club' can mean anything which your family spends money on in the pursuit of a leisure or sporting activity. It could be golf, tennis, cricket, squash, football or anything you care to mention, and as more and more facilities for sport are now being provided, the greater is the likelihood of your family becoming involved in expenditure of one sort or another to cover annual membership fees, purchase of equipment, and playing fees. If the members of your family are not the popular sport-pursuing type, they might go in for quieter pastimes such as wine making, collecting records, painting, etc, which may also require an outlay of money from your family budget.

Membership of any club, professional body or institute inevitably means paying out money on an annually recurring basis, and should be shown on your budget under the months when payments are due. If there is a social side to the club, professional body or institute to which you belong, you will need to decide whether the cost of attending meetings, dinner-dances and similar social events is part of the cost of being a member, or whether it is something which you would do anyway even if you were not a club member, and would therefore come out of the husband's allowance (see page 22) for entertaining or eating out.

Line 24 – Children's sports/hobbies

24	Childrens' sports/ hobbies	15				15				15				45

Your children may well be involved in a sporting activity under the last heading as part of the family's group participation, but in addition may follow their own particular sport and/or hobby. It could be anything – ice skating, dancing or music. All will require a cash allocation in your budget.

Line 25 – Freezer stocks

25	Freezer stocks		30			30			30			30		120

The initial stocking up of a freezer can be an expensive outlay to make, but after you have achieved this the restocking of the freezer could be part of the wife's weekly allowance for food, except for the purchase of large quantities of meat, which will require a substantial payment to be made perhaps four times annually. This is what is shown on this line.

Line 26 – Sundries

26	Sundries			25			25			25			25	100

No budget is complete without an item for 'sundries'. The more comprehensive you make your budget the lower will be the amount you need to allow for 'sundries', but no matter how comprehensive your budget is, there will always be some expense which you had not anticipated and which cannot be allocated to any item other than sundries. You may find, because of your commitments on essential items of your budget, that you can only afford to allocate a very small amount for sundries, or even be tempted to exclude the item entirely. This is not wise because you cannot budget for unexpected events and therefore you must have some money somewhere in your budget which you can call on to deal with or contribute towards the cost of an unexpected event (see page 50).

Line 27 – Total

27	Total expenditure	543	465	410	596	380	385	553	920	463	460	350	533	6060

When you have covered all of your forecasted expenditure, total each line across into the final column, and also vertically, to give monthly totals of expenditure.

Before proceeding to SECTION 3, you should first make comparisons of income and expenditure and, if necessary, make a few adjustments. If the total of your income in the final column of Line 6 is more than the total of your expenditure in the final column of Line 27, then you have succeeded in preparing a satisfactory budget. You may want to leave the cash surplus in the bank, or invest it, or redistribute it on certain items in your budget which you think you may have been mean with and would like to spend more on.

However, if your total forecasted expenditure exceeds your income, then you will either have to trim down your expenditure or increase your income wherever you can, unless of course, you are prepared to overspend on your income, but this means that your money in the bank (assuming that you had some in the bank at the start of your budget) will be reduced by however much you overspend. If you have been honest and accurate in forecasting your expenditure it will not be easy to trim down spending on certain items because usually a large part of your income is already accounted for on such essential items as housekeeping, mortgage, rent, rates, insurance, gas, electricity, etc. Any cutting back on expenditure has to come out of non-essential items and only you can get the priorities right in deciding what is non-essential. There are of course many ways in which it is possible to economise on a wide variety of commodities, and this is dealt with in Chapters 5 and 7. If you can sensibly increase your estimated income then do so, but it would be unwise to increase your forecasted income hoping that somehow you will be able to make extra money or obtain a wage increase to enable you to meet your commitments.

When you have adjusted SECTIONS 1 and 2 of your budget so that INCOME and EXPENDITURE are more or less compatible, you can proceed to the arithmetic of SECTION 3: CONTROL.

Section		Income [1979]	Jan	Feb	Mar	Apr	May	Jun	Jul	Aug	Sep	Oct	Nov	Dec	Total
Section 1	1	Husband	395	395	395	395	395	395	395	395	395	395	395	395	4740
	2	Wife	60	60	60	75	60	60	75	60	75	60	60	75	780
	3	Child benefits	48	48	48	60	48	48	60	48	60	48	48	60	624
	4	Other				10						10			20
	5														
	6	Total income	503	503	503	540	503	503	530	503	530	513	503	530	6164
Section 2		Expenditure				5 weeks			5 weeks		5 weeks			5 weeks	
	7	Husband	72	72	72	90	72	72	90	72	90	72	72	90	936
	8	Wife	120	120	120	150	120	120	150	120	150	120	120	150	1560
	9	Mortgage	50	50	50	50	50	50	50	50	50	50	50	50	600
	10	Ground rent and rates	120	15					100	35					270
	11	Electricity	30			40			20			30			120
	12	Gas			15			15			10			10	50
	13	Telephone	15			20			15			15			65
	14	Heating	35			60			30			15			140
	15	Insurance	8	8	8	20	8	8	8	8	18	8	8	8	118
	16	Television	10	10	10	31	10	10	10	10	10	10	10	10	141
	17	Clothes	20	20	20	25	20	20	25	20	25	20	20	25	260
	18	Car	25	85	25	75	30	25	25	25	25	25	25	25	415
	19	Anniversaries	10		5		10		15	15	5				60
	20	Christmas and holidays		40		20				520				100	680
	21	House and garden maintenance			25			25			25			25	100
	22	Furnishings	15	15	15	15	15	15	15	15	15	15	15	15	180
	23	Sports club			20							80			100
	24	Childrens' sports/ hobbies	15				15				15				45
	25	Freezer stocks		30			30			30			30		120
	26	Sundries			25			25			25			25	100
	27	Total expenditure	545	465	410	596	380	385	553	920	463	460	350	533	6060
Section 3	28	Cumulative income	503	1006	1509	2049	2552	3055	3585	4088	4618	5131	5634	6164	
	29	Cumulative expenditure	545	1010	1420	2016	2396	2781	3334	4254	4717	5177	5527	6060	
	30	Bank Balance Opening Fig £200	158	196	289	233	356	474	451	34	101	154	307	304	
	31	Statement													

Figure 4

Chapter 4

Section 3:

Control of income and expenditure

Even though you may have adjusted SECTIONS 1 and 2 so that your income and expenditure are compatible, you may well find by comparison of some monthly totals that you will be spending more than you will have earned in certain months, e.g. in January, April, July and August in *Figure 4*. This could mean that you are overdrawn at the bank unless in earlier months your forecasted income was more than your forecasted expenditure. That is the object of SECTION 3 – to keep control throughout the year on the running totals of income and expenditure.

Line 28 – Cumulative income

28	Cumulative Income	503	1006	1509	2049	2552	3055	3585	4088	4618	5131	5634	6164	

On this line the total of your monthly income from Line 6 is accumulated month by month so that in the final column of Line 28 the cumulative total is the same as the total in the final column of Line 6.

Line 29 – Cumulative expenditure

29	Cumulative expenditure	545	1010	1420	2016	2396	2781	3334	4254	4717	5177	5527	6060	

Section	Line	Income [1979]	Jan	Feb	Mar	Apr	May	Jun	Jul	Aug	Sep	Oct	Nov	Dec	Total
	1	Husband	395	395	395	395	395	395	395	395	395	395	395	395	4740
	2	Wife	60	60	60	75	60	60	75	60	75	60	60	75	780
	3	Child benefits	48	48	48	60	48	48	60	48	60	48	48	60	624
	4	Other				10						10			20
	5														
Section 1	6	Total income	503	503	503	540	503	503	530	503	530	513	503	530	6164
		Expenditure				5 weeks			5 weeks		5 weeks			5 weeks	
	7	Husband	72	72	72	90	72	72	90	72	90	72	72	90	936
	8	Wife	120	120	120	150	120	120	150	120	150	120	120	150	1560
	9	Mortgage	50	50	50	50	50	50	50	50	50	50	50	50	600
	10	Ground rent and rates	36	31	16	16	16	16	16	51	16	16	16	24	270
	11	Electricity	10	10	10	10	10	10	10	10	10	10	10	10	120
	12	Gas	4	4	4	4	4	4	4	4	4	4	4	6	50
	13	Telephone	15			20			15			15			65
	14	Heating	12	12	12	12	12	12	12	12	12	12	12	8	140
	15	Insurance	8	8	8	20	8	8	8	8	18	8	8	8	118
	16	Television	10	10	10	31	10	10	10	10	10	10	10	10	141
	17	Clothes	20	20	20	25	20	20	25	20	25	20	20	25	260
	18	Car	25	85	25	75	30	25	25	25	25	25	25	25	415
	19	Anniversaries	10		5		10		15	15	5				60
	20	Christmas and holidays		40		20				520				100	680
	21	House and garden maintenance			25			25			25			25	100
	22	Furnishings	15	15	15	15	15	15	15	15	15	15	15	15	180
	23	Sports club			20							80			100
	24	Childrens' sports/hobbies	15				15				15				45
	25	Freezer stocks		30			30			30			30		120
	26	Sundries			25			25			25			25	100
Section 2	27	Totai expenditure	422	507	437	538	422	412	445	962	495	457	392	571	6060
	28	Cumulative Income	503	1006	1509	2049	2552	3055	3585	4088	4618	5131	5634	6164	
	29	Cumulative expenditure	422	929	1366	1904	2326	2738	3183	4145	4640	5097	5489	6060	
	30	Bank Balance Opening Fig £200	281	277	343	345	426	517	602	143	178	234	345	304	
Section 3	31	Statement													

Figure 5 (Same budget as Figure 4 but with costs on Lines 10, 11, 12 and 14 spread over 12 months)

Similarly on this line your total monthly expenditure is accumulated month by month so that in the final column the cumulative total is the same as the total in the final column of Line 27. By comparing the monthly totals on Lines 28 and 29 you will be able to see directly whether your budget is working to plan. So long as your forecasted INCOME and forecasted EXPENDITURE are compatible at the end of the year, you can be confident that any forecasted overspending in any particular month will have been corrected by the end of the year.

If you are worried about the accumulation of heavy expenditure in certain months, which is caused by the simultaneous arrival of several large bills, then there are easy payment schemes available at most local authority, gas and electricity board offices. Many banks also offer a similar service which covers as many items as you wish to have paid on an instalment basis. The service is not necessarily provided free of charge, so when enquiring about these schemes be sure to ask about charges – interest or otherwise – for the service (see example on page 89).

It does mean in certain circumstances that initially you have to pay your last quarterly bill and then start paying towards the next one immediately afterwards. Again make sure that you understand what is required from you when converting the manner in which you make payments on your budget sheet. Assuming that you have accounted for the initial cost of converting from quarterly payment to monthly instalment payment, you can see in *Figure 5* how the same budget as *Figure 4* works out, when the costs on Lines 10, 11, 12 and 14 are spread out over a period of twelve months. The balance at the bank on Line 30 over the year looks much healthier even though the result at the year end is the same. One illuminating point about the *Figure 5* budget is that the holiday costing £520.00 could now be taken in June or July, whereas in the *Figure 4* budget the holiday cannot be afforded any earlier than August.

Line 30 – Bank balance

30	Bank Balance Opening Fig £200	158	196	289	233	356	474	451	34	101	154	307	304	

If you are overspending on your income, this will show on Line 30 (it will also show if you are underspending, but be thankful – that is no cause for concern) and it means that you are drawing money from the bank (provided you have some in the bank).

To calculate the figures on Line 30 (*Figure 4*) you need to know how much money you have in the bank at the commencement of your budget period. Make sure that the figure you use is adjusted to (*a*) be clear of all payments prior to your budget period; (*b*) take into account any payments from your budget which you have already made. Otherwise you will never get the figures on Lines 30 and 31 compatible. If you do not have any money in the bank then you must ensure that your monthly income always exceeds, or is at least equal to, your monthly expenditure, otherwise you will be in trouble with your bank manager unless you have a prior overdraft arrangement with him.

Having established the proper figure to commence with, the figures in Line 30 are arrived at by taking the difference between the figures on Line 6 and Line 27 and either adding or subtracting from the 'Balance at bank', depending on whether you have earned more than you have spent in that particular month, or vice versa. For example, if you start the year with £200.00 (as on Line 30 of the example in *Figure 4*) and your January income is £42.00 less than your January expenses, then your bank balance will go down by £42.00 to £158.00. If in February your monthly income is £38.00 more than your monthly expenses, then your bank balance will go up by £38.00 to £196.00. If you repeat this for every month of the year you will be able to see at a glance how much money you can expect to have in the bank at any month end during the year.

One of the aims of your first budget should be to save some of your income so that you can build up a working fund to start off your next budget with. This will enable you to cope with the months when your expenses exceed your income, without embarrassment at the bank, but in addition to this it is advisable that your family should save some of their income for a 'rainy day'. If you look through the check list at the end of this book you are sure to see several items or events which will certainly enter into one of your budgets at some time in the future, eg more and more children go on to further or higher education before they start earning a wage, and daughters have the habit of getting married. So it is worthwhile striving to save some money for yourself or your family. There is no reason why, if you can afford it, that you should not have a line in SECTION 2 of your budget for 'savings', on which you can show how much of your income you would like to put away regularly each month for savings.

Alternatively you may want your savings to earn some more INCOME for you by way of investment. There are many ways of saving and investing money to choose from, but generally speaking the ways of investing money which earn a good return and at the same time ensure that your savings are not devalued by inflation have high risks attached to them. Investment with less associated risks may show a lesser return but your money is usually much safer. If you want advice on this your bank manager will be able to help you, or you can learn more on this subject by reading Gordon Cumming's *The Complete Guide to Investment* (published by Penguin Books). You may of course wish to invest your money in property, jewellery, precious stones/metals, antiques and similar items which are likely to appreciate in value over the years.

Line 31 – Statement

31	Statement													

To be sure you have not overlooked a payment of income or expenditure, you can check your calculations of your bank balance by asking your bank to let you have 'regular end of the month statements' of your current account. The figures on the statement for each month end should be the same as your figure at each month end on Line 31.

If they are not the same, check through the bank statement to ensure that the bank has cleared all of the cheques you have paid in and out during the month. Check also that you have accounted for all of your outgoing payments in your entries for each month as it is easy to overlook such things as 'standing order' payments, interest and bank charges. This task will be made simpler if you have a joint current account, as all of your outgoing payments will appear on one 'end of the month statement'. You may have difficulty in reconciling Line 30 with Line 31 when you receive your 'end of the month statement' of your current account from the bank. Do not be too concerned if you cannot reconcile the two figures exactly – it is better to have a budget with the arithmetic slightly incorrect than have no budget at all.

Chapter 5

Your budget in operation – and what happens if it goes wrong

When your budget period has expired, it should look something like *Figure 6* with all your income and expenditure recorded in red ink (shown by grey shading). To achieve this you must consistently fill in your income and expenditure at the end of each month. Look through the counterfoils of your cheque books and summarise the amounts you have spent on the various items of your budget. Add to these amounts any 'standing order' payments, interest earned or charged and any other earnings or charges. If you have only a few payments to pay out each month then you probably will be able to summarise them on a piece of convenient scrap paper. If, however, you have a full budget, with lots of items requiring a number of payments to be made each month, you may need to have a monthly summary sheet similar to *Figure 7*, to keep track of your payments. This sheet is also useful if you are interested in keeping a more detailed record of your expenditure.

If you look at *Figure 7* you will see that the headings across the top of the sheet are the same as those on the budget sheet in *Figure 6*, but as an example of the sort of additional information which can be provided, the amounts spent on Lines 17 and 18 (Clothes and Car) have been sub-divided to show how the amount on the budget sheet has been arrived at.

At the end of each month the expenditure under each heading is totalled, but before entering these summarised amounts on your budget

Section	No.	Income [1979]	Jan	Feb	Mar	Apr	May	Jun	Jul	Aug	Sep	Oct	Nov	Dec	Total
Section 1	1	Husband	395	395	395	395	395	395	395	395	395	395	395	395	4740
			395	395	394	394	396	396	426	426	425	425	425	475	4972
	2	Wife	60	60	60	75	60	60	75	60	75	60	60	75	780
			58	56	59	74	60	61	74	59	74	59	60	80	774
	3	Child benefits	48	48	48	60	48	48	60	48	60	48	48	60	624
			48	48	48	60	48	48	60	48	60	48	48	60	624
	4	Other				10						10			20
							11			15		8			34
	5														
	6	Total income	503	503	503	540	503	503	530	503	530	513	503	530	6164
			501	499	501	528	515	505	560	548	559	540	533	615	6404
Section 2		Expenditure				5 weeks			5 weeks		5 weeks			5 weeks	
	7	Husband	72	72	72	90	72	72	90	72	90	72	72	90	936
			72	83	95	105	80	72	90	102	93	70	75	110	1047
	8	Wife	120	120	120	150	120	120	150	120	150	120	120	150	1560
			120	120	120	160	120	120	150	130	150	130	120	170	1610
	9	Mortgage	50	50	50	50	50	50	50	50	50	50	50	50	600
			50	50	50	50	50	50	50	50	50	50	50	50	600
	10	Ground rent and rates	120	15					100	35					270
				120	15				100	20	15				270
	11	Electricity	30			40			20			30			120
			40			35			25			36			136
	12	Gas			15			15			10			10	50
					14			18			12			15	59
	13	Telephone	15			20			15			15			65
			13			21			16			13			63
	14	Heating	35			60			30			15			140
				32		63			40				16		151
	15	Insurance	8	8	8	20	8	8	8	8	18	8	8	8	118
			8	8	8	20	8	8	8	8	18	8	8	8	118
	16	Television	10	10	10	31	10	10	10	10	10	10	10	10	141
			10	10	10	31	10	10	10	10	10	10	10	10	141
	17	Clothes	20	20	20	25	20	20	25	20	25	20	20	25	260
			10		35	12	22	60	16	6	8	35	9	10	223
	18	Car	25	85	25	75	30	25	25	25	25	25	25	25	415
			21	75	15	75	31	21	19	17	10	85	22	28	419
	19	Anniversaries	10		5		10		15	15	5				60
			8		7		12		22	10		6			65
	20	Christmas and holidays		40		20				520				100	680
				40		25				580				105	750
	21	House and garden maintenance			25			25			25			25	100
				15				30	10			18	8		81
	22	Furnishings	15	15	15	15	15	15	15	15	15	15	15	15	180
					45		20	15	15	17			32	40	169
	23	Sports club			20							80			100
						23						85			108
	24	Childrens' sports/ hobbies	15				15				15				45
			15				15					15			45
	25	Freezer stocks		30			30			30			30		120
				25				30						40	95
	26	Sundries			25			25			25			25	100
				10			30	10	5			119	8		182
	27	Total expenditure	545	465	410	596	380	385	553	920	463	460	350	533	6060
			367	588	414	620	398	444	578	933	366	712	326	586	6332
Section 3	28	Cumulative Income	503	1006	1509	2049	2552	3055	3585	4088	4618	5131	5634	6164	
			501	1000	1501	2029	2544	3049	3609	4157	4716	5255	5789	6404	
	29	Cumulative expenditure	545	1010	1420	2016	2396	2781	3334	4254	4717	5177	5527	6060	
			367	955	1369	1989	2387	2831	3409	4342	4708	5420	5746	6332	
	30	Bank Balance Opening Fig £200	158	196	289	233	356	474	451	34	101	154	307	304	
			334	245	332	240	357	418	400	15	208	36	243	272	
	31	Statement													
			330	248	325	239	357	424	403	10	200	35	249	272	

Figure 6

sheet, check through the husband's and wife's cash allowance to pick out any item for which you may have paid cash out of your pocket on other items in your budget. For instance if you withdrew £10.00 cash as part of the husband's allowance and he bought a £6.00 shirt out of that money then, by making a note to that effect on the counterfoil of the £10.00 withdrawal in your cheque book, you can keep the husband's cash allowance and the amount spent on clothing in perspective.

Similarly, if you pay money out of your own pocket for which you are later reimbursed by your employer or someone else, be careful how you account for this money in your budget. For example you may buy petrol for your car and recover the money later as part of your expenses from your employer. If after recovering the money you spend it on yourself, the money should be entered in your budget sheet, not as part of the cost of running your car, but as part of your cash allowance.

When you have made these adjustments enter the summarised figures on your budget sheet. You will find this information invaluable in preparing your next budget – as you will in all succeeding budgets. Once you have got into the habit of making helpful notes on the counterfoils of your cheque book you will find that filling in your month-end figures on your budget sheet will take fifteen minutes at the most.

If you purchase any goods or services using a credit card (Access/Barclaycard or other) or by mail order, you may have a few problems in sorting out how you account for this expenditure on your budget sheet. Say you bought clothing to the value of £50.00 using your credit card. The minimum payments required by the bank would be demanded monthly and each payment you make would be entered on Line 17, Clothes. If three months later you purchased a piece of furniture for £75.00, and a month after that you paid £50.00 for car repairs, these amounts would be added to the balance unpaid on the clothing bought earlier – plus interest. The bank would continue to send you demands for increased monthly payments which would be partly on account of the furniture and car repairs. You have then to sort out the proportion of the monthly payments which are to be allocated to the three separate items on your budget sheet. This is not too difficult but you must keep a record of when you finish paying for the first item – clothes – and then the second item – furniture – and then the car repairs.

Summary of monthly expenditure   * Denotes 'standing order payment'   Year 1979

Line	7	8	9	10	11	12	13	14	15	16	17	17	17	18	18	18	19	20	21	22	23	24	25	26	
											Clothing			Car											
Date / Item	Husband	Wife	Mortgage *	Rates	Electricity	Gas	Phone	Heating	Insurance *	Television *	Husbnd	Wife	Childn	Petrol	Tax & insrnce	Serv & repairs	Annivs	Christmas Holidays	House & garden	Furnishings	Sports club	Childrens' hobbies	Freezer	Sundries	Remarks
JAN 3	15													5											
7		30															4								John's birthday
10	18																								
14		30																							
15					40								10	5			..								Ann & Jill's shoes
21	15	30																							
23							13										4								Jill's birthday
25									8	10				5											
27	11		50											6											
28		30											10	21								15			
31	13																								
TOTAL	72	120	50		40		13		8	10		10			21		8					15			
FEB 1	18			100																					
4		30												3											
7				20											60										Car insurance
10	15																								
11		30						32						5									25		Freezer meat
17	18																	40							Hols Deposit
18		30												3											
25	21	30	50						8	10				4					15						Paint & paper bedroom
28	11													15	60										
																								10	Dentist
TOTAL	83	120	50	120				32	8	10					75			40	15				25	10	

Figure 7

One solution is to keep all of your bank's demand slips so that you have a record of your payments in the same way as you would when buying from a mail order firm and paying weekly instalments.

You may think this to be unimportant, and that as long as you account for your expenditure somewhere it does not really matter. It matters when you are preparing a succeeding budget and you are trying to establish how much you spent on what in the previous year.

What happens if your budget goes wrong?

The sample family budget used in this book is a successful one, because it ended up showing more money in the bank than at the start of the year (even though not as much as was forecasted – see *Figure 6*, Line 30). It represents a hypothetical family, which has been fairly well organised. With experience there is no reason why your own budget should not be equally as successful – but not every time. Something somewhere will go wrong sometime. Your budget can go off-course for any number of reasons, but generally speaking they will all fall into one of two categories.

1 **Miscalculation of forecasted known income and/or expenditure** You have either underestimated your general expenditure or you have overestimated your income. The only remedy for this situation is to draw up a revised budget forecast commencing with the financial situation as it actually exists, and using revised earning and spending figures as you actually know them to be. The same principles which applied to your previous budget will apply to your revised budget – at the end the figures on Lines 28 and 29 must be compatible; otherwise you will soon be back in financial difficulties. To produce a satisfactory revised budget may mean, not only cutting down on expenditure, but cutting out some items entirely, eg holidays, sport, leisure or motor car. The order of priority for such action will be that which is least painful for the family. As an example of a fairly painless exercise in cutting down expenditure, suppose in *Figure 6* a speeding fine of £50.00 had to be paid in July, a month when there is already heavy expenditure, followed by a month when

there is even heavier expenditure. The situation is made worse because, looking at the figures in the shaded column on Line 30 for the month of June, the balance at the bank is actually £56.00 less than the forecasted amount (in ordinary type), but there is still just enough money in the bank to meet the forecasted spending in the following months of July and August. However, we have got to find £50.00 to pay the speeding fine in July which means that the balance at the bank would be £50.00 overdrawn in August unless we cut down the spending in July and August by £50.00. This could have been possible by reducing expenditure as follows:

	July	August	Total reduction
Line 17 Clothes	£10.00	£5.00	£15.00
Line 18 Car	£10.00	£5.00	£15.00
Line 22 Furnishings	£5.00	£5.00	£10.00
Line 25 Freezer		£10.00	£10.00
			£50.00

or

2 **The occurrence of an unexpected event or events**
How you cope with this depends on the magnitude of the costs associated with the unexpected event, and also when the event happens. If it occurs early in your budget period you may have time to absorb the cost by trimming down on your non-essential spending, but if the event happens later in your budget period it could be more of a problem, because you may have used up your reserves and have little to spare from your non-essential spending. This does not necessarily mean that a cash crisis has to be resolved within the period which your present budget covers. It is better if you can, but if you cannot, extend your budget period into the next six, nine or twelve months to see if you can work yourself out of debt in that time. The first thing to do if you have a costly unexpected event, or if

you have made a serious miscalculation, is to look closely at Line 30 on your budget sheet. You may or may not have sufficient cash to deal with the unexpected cost in the month in which it occurs, but if you do deal with the crisis in that month make sure that you are not causing an even more severe cash crisis in a later month, when your forecasted bank balance is already low. This is when overspending will hit you the hardest and this is the time to anticipate how you will cope with the crisis. If you have no surplus cash or insufficient cash anywhere on Line 30 to cope with the crisis, then the only way you can meet the unexpected expenditure is to do one of the following:

a Cut down on your expenditure
b Raise extra cash without borrowing
c Borrow the money

a *Cutting down your expenditure* means making sacrifices by going without something from the unexpired part of your budget. You can only cut down on non-essential spending because such things as mortgage/rent, rates, gas, electricity, insurance, etc, still have to be paid, and payment cannot be put off indefinitely. There is a sensible limit to the amount which you can cut down on non-essential spending. Cutting down on expenditure is dealt with in the following chapter, but obviously the items to cut down on are those which you are spending the most money on. What are the large items in your budget which you could say are non-essential? Using the sample budget shown in *Figure 8*, what would you do to reduce expenditure on non-essential items?

Large items in order of magnitude

i *Husband's and wife's allowances (Lines 7 and 8) – £2496.00*
Some of this expenditure is non-essential.
Remember the lists on page 22?

Husband	*Wife*
Smoking	All food (excluding large purchases of meat for freezer)
Entertaining	

Husband	*Wife*
Drinking	Toiletries, kitchen and other
Eating out	consumable household goods
Newspapers	School meals and bus fares
Children's pocket money	Hairdressing and cosmetics
Theatre/cinema	

Certainly there are a number of items here which could be cut out or reduced.

ii *Holidays (Line 20) cost – £520.00*
Can the holiday be cancelled? Does it have to be cancelled entirely? Can a cheaper form of holiday be taken?

iii *Car (Line 18) cost – £415.00*
Can the car be used less or at a cost which is less than using an alternative means of transport?

iv *Small items*

		Cost
Line 13	Telephone	£65.00
Line 14	Heating	£140.00
Line 17	Clothes	£260.00
Line 21	House and garden maintenance	£100.00
Line 22	Furnishings	£180.00
Line 23	Sports Club	£100.00
Line 24	Children's sport/hobby	£45.00
Line 26	Sundries	£100.00

Can any of this expenditure be avoided or reduced? If after you have fully considered all possible reductions in the budget you are still looking for large sums of money, you will have to consider one of the alternative means of solving the cash crisis discussed in the following paragraphs (b) or (c).

b *Raise some money by selling some of your belongings*, eg jewellery, furniture, clothing, property, shares, car, etc. In this way there are

Section		Income [1979]	Jan	Feb	Mar	Apr	May	Jun	Jul	Aug	Sep	Oct	Nov	Dec	Total
Section 1	1	Husband	395	395	395	395	395	395	395	395	395	395	395	395	4740
Section 1	2	Wife	60	60	60	75	60	60	75	60	75	60	60	75	780
Section 1	3	Child benefits	48	48	48	60	48	48	60	48	60	48	48	60	624
Section 1	4	Other				10						10			20
Section 1	5														
Section 1	6	Total income	503	503	503	540	503	503	530	503	530	513	503	530	6164
Section 2		Expenditure				5 weeks			5 weeks		5 weeks			5 weeks	
Section 2	7	Husband	72	72	72	90	72	72	90	72	90	72	72	90	936
Section 2	8	Wife	120	120	120	150	120	120	150	120	150	120	120	150	1560
Section 2	9	Mortgage	50	50	50	50	50	50	50	50	50	50	50	50	600
Section 2	10	Ground rent and rates	120	15					100	35					270
Section 2	11	Electricity	30			40			20			30			120
Section 2	12	Gas			15			15			10			10	50
Section 2	13	Telephone	15			20			15			15			65
Section 2	14	Heating	35			60			30			15			140
Section 2	15	Insurance	8	8	8	20	8	8	8	8	18	8	8	8	118
Section 2	16	Television	10	10	10	31	10	10	10	10	10	10	10	10	141
Section 2	17	Clothes	20	20	20	25	20	20	25	20	25	20	20	25	260
Section 2	18	Car	25	85	25	75	30	25	25	25	25	25	25	25	415
Section 2	19	Anniversaries	10		5		10		15	15	5				60
Section 2	20	Christmas and holidays		40		20				520				100	680
Section 2	21	House and garden maintenance			25			25			25			25	100
Section 2	22	Furnishings	15	15	15	15	15	15	15	15	15	15	15	15	180
Section 2	23	Sports club			20							80			100
Section 2	24	Childrens' sports/ hobbies	15				15				15				45
Section 2	25	Freezer stocks		30			30			30			30		120
Section 2	26	Sundries			25			25			25			25	100
Section 2	27	Total expenditure	545	465	410	596	380	385	553	920	463	460	350	533	6060
Section 3	28	Cumulative Income	503	1006	1509	2049	2552	3055	3585	4088	4618	5131	5634	6164	
Section 3	29	Cumulative expenditure	545	1010	1420	2016	2396	2781	3334	4254	4717	5177	5527	6060	
Section 3	30	Bank Balance Opening Fig £200	158	196	289	233	356	474	451	34	101	154	307	304	
Section 3	31	Statement													

Figure 8

no repayments to be accounted for out of your budget and provided that sufficient money is raised not too painfully, it is an effective way of dealing with a cash crisis and restoring your budget to an even keel. Taking on additional part-time work may help you to raise extra cash, but if you need a large amount quickly this may not be the answer. However, if you have to raise money by way of a loan described in the following paragraph (c), part-time working could be a way of repaying the loan by instalments.

c *Borrow the money*. It is not always easy to borrow money and there are no hard and fast rules or conditions by which you can determine whether or not you can borrow money from any particular source. The availability of money and the willingness of money lenders to let you borrow money from them has as much to do with the prevailing national and international economic climate as it has with your rating as a person to whom credit facilities can be allowed. Let us just say that there are times when it is easy to borrow money, and there are times when it is very difficult; and you will either be lucky or unlucky depending on the money lending climate at the time you need to borrow some.

If you can borrow the money it will mean having to revise your budget to account for the inevitable repayment of the loan, plus any interest, either by instalments or as a single lump sum payment. Repayment by instalments will not have as severe an effect on your revised budget as would a single lump sum repayment, but the severity of the effect on your budget depends on the type and terms of the loan you take. Having an *overdraft* at your bank is a loan and you may be on sufficiently good terms with your bank manager for him to allow you to overspend on your budget up to a certain limit. He will of course want to look at your budget sheet and be satisfied that you have the means to repay the overdraft within that time limit. The disadvantage of this is that the bank can call on you to repay the loan at any time they think it is necessary to do so. In these circumstances you find yourself back in the same cash crisis as you were prior to having an overdraft. If you require a large amount of money you will probably have to look for a loan with repayments over a *long term* (five to twenty-five years) so that the amount of the repayment instalment is small and easier to accommodate within your budget. The alternative is to seek a *short term* loan, which usually means repayment within a maximum period of five years. Therefore the amount of money which you can borrow for a short term is determined by deciding whether you can afford to pay each repayment which the sum you are borrowing mathematically demands over the term for which the money is being borrowed. If you cannot afford the repayments over five years then you must consider a long term loan. Both sorts of loan are considered in more detail in the paragraphs which follow.

A *short term loan* used to mean a maximum period of three years but more recently this has been extended to five years by some money lending sources. It may be possible for you to arrange a *private loan* from someone you know, such as a close relative or friend, or even your employer, either with or without interest depending on the closeness of the relationship between the parties concerned. Even so it is preferable that the amount of the loan, and the terms of repayment, are clearly understood and defined in writing so that in the event of a subsequent dispute neither party can default or be placed in unnecessary distress. There are, of course, finance companies and other money lenders from whom you could take a private personal loan, but their interest charges and terms of repayment will not usually be as competitive as a loan from the bank or Building Society, so try asking them for a loan first. If you have no choice but to borrow from a finance company or private money lender then you would be wise to take professional advice from a solicitor or accountant before entering into a formal agreement to borrow money in this way. If you cannot arrange a *private personal loan*, approach your bank manager for a *bank personal loan*. If he is willing to let you borrow the money it will be only on the bank's own terms and again you would be wise to take professional advice on the terms offered.

Whether you take a *private personal loan* or a *bank personal loan* the money lender will require some form of security against which the money can be loaned and which will more than adequately pay back the money lender if he has to dispose of that security in order to recoup whatever money is outstanding in the event of the borrower defaulting in repayment of the loan. Security for the money lender may take the form of property, shares or an insurance policy. In the case of the latter, if there is a sizeable cash-in value, your insurance company may give you a loan, using the cash-in value as security.

Long term loans are generally more suited to Building Societies and can usually only be taken by those owning property. If you own property which is not already mortgaged or has a small mortgage on it which is for an amount much less than the market value of the property, you may be able to obtain a second mortgage, repayable over a long term. In this way the repayments would be small compared with a short term loan, and therefore much easier to accommodate within your budget. In addition you will be able to claim tax relief on the money borrowed against your home. If you own a fairly new property, which has a mortgage in your name, and you have carried out certain improvements which you think have considerably increased the market value of the property, you may be able to borrow long term money against that increase in the value of your property. The Building Society (or your bank if you are looking for a five year loan) will need to be satisfied that the increased value does exist and for this purpose they will employ a surveyor to assess the new market value of the property. You may have to pay the surveyor's fee beforehand, so enquire with your Building Society how much the fee will be, and also the legal costs of employing a solicitor to act on your behalf in the second mortgage transaction.

If after you have thoroughly investigated all avenues, your financial problems are not entirely resolved, do not wait until your creditors close in on you, demanding their money, because once they do this it is more difficult to persuade them to withdraw. Work out how much you can afford to pay weekly to the people to whom you owe money, and write to them explaining your difficulties and the amount you can afford to pay them each week until your debt is cleared. They may be prepared to accept your proposals for repayment – remember they are more interested in getting their money back than suing you – but even if they are not as satisfied as they might be, a compromise solution may be possible.

Chapter 6

Anticipating and forecasting future expenditure

When you have seen your first budget period through and you are thinking about the preparation of your next budget, you might be inclined to build your new budget around your previous one, using the same items with updated cost forecasts. The danger is that you may overlook an item which, although not on your last budget sheet, should be included in your new budget. If you look through the Check List on pages 95–96 there will certainly be some items which will eventually appear in one of your future budgets. Quite a few of the items will not concern you at all, but some of them could have a very significant effect on your budget. This chapter is a selection of some of the significant milestones from the Check List, with a few helpful notes for your guidance in accommodating each item within your budget.

Baby

It is quite feasible that after you have prepared your budget, and before it expires, a baby could be conceived and born into the family – causing all sorts of problems in your budget, not only in the form of additional expenditure but possibly a substantial loss of income previously provided by the mother. A new baby need not of course be an unexpected event, but whether it was expected or not the effect on your budget will be the same. If the wife is working and earning a wage you will need to determine when she has to give up her job to have the baby. Her income, if any, will disappear from your budget, but there will be other income in the form of Maternity Benefits and a grant to add back into your budget (provided that you can satisfy certain conditions regarding payment of National Insurance contributions). This is explained in Leaflet NI 17A, available from your local Social Security offices. Rates of benefit can be found in Leaflet NI 196, also available from your local Social Security offices. There will be tax benefits made to the husband's income and there will also be Child Benefits to add to income. It will probably be necessary to revise your budget, adjusting not only your income but expenditure also.

You could be faced with initial expenditure on new clothing and equipment in the order of

	£
Mother's maternity wear	90
Baby's clothing	50
Baby's equipment	80
	220

but you may not necessarily need all of this clothing and equipment by virtue of hand-me-downs, gifts and loaned equipment. Therefore the above information can be used for guidance only, but if you are expecting a baby in the family or if you are planning to have one in the near future, it is essential that you revise your budget as quickly as possible to ensure that you can cope with the loss (if any) of income, and that you can meet the new expenditure when the baby arrives.

Education

The cost of educating your child or children, unless you decide to pay for private education, is provided largely by the state out of the taxes and rates contributed by the populace. Nevertheless there will be some costs which you will have to pay yourself, and as these costs can sometimes be considerable it is advisable to try to make an assessment before making your budget forecast.

Up to the age of five years your child may attend nursery school, provided there is one in your locality, and that there is a place available. The alternative is attendance at a playgroup or nursery, but you will usually have to pay for attendance at either, if they are run privately, to cover the cost of hiring the premises, insurance, milk, paid supervisors and equipment. Therefore, the fees will vary depending on the facilities provided, and you will need to make enquiries regarding the expenditure in advance of preparing your budget.

When your child starts infant school at the age of five, the only expenses you will be concerned with will be fares, school meals, purchase of uniform, equipment for sporting pursuits, any special books or stationery, school visits, and extra school curricula. Not all schools have or insist on a school uniform but if your child is expected to wear a uniform, here is a typical list of clothing and equipment which you may be expected to provide.

Boy

Blazer	Overcoat	Football boots
Trousers	Scarf	Plimsolls
Shirt	Satchel	Towel
Pullover	Overall	Swimming trunks
Tie	Vest	Duffel bag
Socks	Shorts	Track suit
Shoes	Football shirt	Training shoes
Raincoat	Football socks	

Girl

Blazer	Overcoat	Games socks
Skirt	Scarf	Games shoes
Blouse	Satchel	Plimsolls
Cardigan	Apron	Towel
Tie	Summer dress	Swimming suit
Socks	Leotard	Duffel bag
Shoes	Games skirt	Track suit
Raincoat	Games blouse	Hockey stick

If you delete the non-compulsory items from this list and put an approximate price against the remaining items you will be very lucky if the total cost is less than £55.00 per child. It may be possible to minimise expenditure with hand-me-down clothing and equipment, but remember that you may have to buy several uniforms during your children's school years by virtue of their growth and change of schools. If you decide to have your child educated at a private school then in addition to the above expenditure there will be fees to account for in your budget. There is no set scale of charges for private schooling – you get what you pay for – and that means that if the school provides lots of facilities and has a good academic record it will be expensive, and vice versa.

When your children reach school leaving age there may still be the cost of further education, or higher education coupled with apprenticeship or other career training to account for in your budget. You may have to pay this cost yourself but often the costs will be met by an employer or contributed towards by way of a grant from the government.

Wedding

If you have a forthcoming marriage in your family you will need to determine at an early stage who is paying for what, because the tradition of the bride's family paying for most of the wedding costs is not necessarily followed these days. Particularly if one family wants to have a big wedding and the other family only wants a small wedding, then the respective families may agree to share the cost between them. Needless to say the cost of a wedding is influenced by the type of ceremony, the number of invited guests, form of dress and honeymoon.

Your wedding budget layout might look something like *Figure 9* (insert your own expenses):

Homebuying

If you are contemplating your first house purchase and have ascertained how much money you can borrow, and therefore how much the mortgage repayment would be, this amount is simply substituted in your

Figure 9. Wedding

Item	*Bride*	*Bride's family*	*Groom*	*Groom's family*	*Total*
Engagement ring					
Wedding ring					
Marriage Licence					
Marriage Certificate					
Church					
(i) Use of					
(ii) Choir					
(iii) Organ					
(iv) Bells					
(v) Tip for verger					
Taxis/hired cars					
Flowers					
Bridesmaids'					
Dresses					
Presents					
Bride's					
Wedding Dress					
Going away outfit					
Groom's outfit					
Hire of morning dress					
Wedding cake					
Guests' cake boxes					
Reception					
Drinks before meal					
wine					
liqueur					
Food					
Music					
Flowers					
Hire of premises					
Decorations					
After reception					
Music					
Food and drinks					
Invitations and postage					
Table place cards					
Newspaper announcement					
Photographer					
Honeymoon					
Total					

budget for the rent, if any, paid on Line 9 prior to the purchase of the house. In addition there will be other costs connected with the house purchase which you will need to anticipate in your budget as follows:

a **Surveyor's fees** – before the Building Society, or whoever you are borrowing the money from, will advance you the money, they will need to satisfy themselves that the property is worth what you have agreed to pay, and also that it is, or will be, soundly constructed. Therefore they will engage a surveyor, on whom they can rely to submit a thorough report, to carry out a survey on their behalf. You have to pay for this service and the charge varies according to the type, age and value of the property. Your Building Society will tell you what the approximate cost will be, if you enquire beforehand.

b **Legal expenses** – you will need the services of a solicitor or other similar professional adviser to deal with the actual purchase of the property from the present owner. The fee for this service is made up for performing the duties listed below, the charge for which varies according to different scales, conditions and the complexity of the purchase:

i Making searches and enquiries to ensure that the title to the property is free from defects, restrictive covenants, etc. Dealing with the transfer of the property into your name and providing the necessary documents.

ii Dealing with the Building Society or money lender for paying out your money.

iii Payment of Land Registry fees – these vary according to the value of the property, and whether or not it was previously unregistered.

iv Payment of Stamp Duty – this is only paid on property over a certain value and then on a scale related to the purchase price.

Your solicitor will give you advice as to the likely cost of his services.

c **Estate Agent's fees** – Similarly if you are selling your present property and purchasing another one, then you can expect to meet the above charges plus, possibly, Estate Agent's and advertising costs in connection with the sale of your existing home. Estate Agent's fees are usually based on a percentage of about $1\frac{1}{2}$ per cent to 2 per cent of the sale price of the property plus the actual cost of any press or other advertising.

d **Professional fees** – If you are having a new house built to your own design or having an existing home altered and extended, you may require the services of an architect and, if the work is very large or complex, perhaps also a structural engineer and quantity surveyor. Although each profession has its own scale of charges, all related to the cost of the building works, you would be wise to agree a fixed sum with each party for their respective services, which is only varied if the original design works are extensively varied. If, however, the extensions and alterations you require are very small, you may only need the less expensive services of a draughtsman/surveyor with a knowledge of obtaining the necessary Planning Consent and Building Regulation Approval.

e **Home improvement grants** – If your property was built before 2 October 1961 and is in need of considerable renovation and improvements, you may be entitled to financial assistance from the government, towards the cost of certain works. If you think you are entitled to a grant, there is a booklet published by the Department of the Environment called *Your Guide to House Renovation Grants*. This gives guidance as to how to obtain the grants, but Circular 160/74, Housing Act 1974 *Improvement of Older Housing* (available from HMSO) gives more information about the Act.

f **Removals and storage** – If you are moving to accommodation fairly near to your present abode, there should not be a great deal of difference in removal costs charged by local removal firms, but a firm looking for work will always be more competitive than one which has plenty of business on. If you want to get the best deal for yourself invite a few removal companies to give you a quotation for packing (if required) and removing all of your belongings to your new address.

Alternatively consider hiring a van locally and do the removal job yourself, with help from your family and friends, otherwise the removal work might become protracted, and with time off work, loss of earnings, etc, it may turn out to be more expensive than employing a removals contractor. If you are moving a long distance it is worthwhile sending out a few more enquiries, not just to local removal firms, but farther afield, as you may be lucky enough to find a firm looking for a return load which should make their estimate much more competitive.

Health

Everyone is entitled to free treatment for ill health in this country, subject to certain qualifications and the payment of prescription charges in certain instances. If this is all you ever require from the National Health Service, then you will not be concerned with great expenditure in respect of your health. However, if you are not satisfied with the National Heath Service and you seek something better, then you will have to pay for it by way of private treatment. There are several private patients insurance schemes, eg BUPA. Again you get what you pay for, which means that benefits receivable are related to the subscriptions you pay. Sometimes you can receive treatment at preferential rates. For example if your employer makes contributions on your behalf for private health treatment, you can usually extend that treatment to cover the entire family at greatly reduced cost.

Similarly with eye, teeth and ear treatment, the National Health offer a service either free or at reduced cost, but if you are not satisfied with their highest standards then you can take private treatment at your own expense. For instance you may not like the choice of National Health Service spectacles, hearing aids or dentures; but something better will probably cost you more money.

Redundancy

Being made redundant or volunteering for redundancy can be a significant milestone in your life. To some people the business of having to adapt and re-train for a new career, always assuming that one can be found, can be a traumatic experience. If you have difficulty in finding another job or source of income, this calls for very careful budgeting to ensure that your redundancy and unemployment benefit money is used to maximum effect and covers your expenditure for as long a period as possible. This will give you an indication of the amount of time you can afford to wait for the right job to come along for you, but obviously you will want to be back in employment as quickly as possible, so that you can retain as much of your savings/redundancy money as possible for better use. To other people, however, being made redundant can be the best thing that ever happened to them. Often the redundancy payment can provide sufficient capital and incentive to go into business on your own account and to others who have no difficulty in finding alternative employment the redundancy payment becomes a useful sum, perhaps permitting a much sought-after holiday, motor car, home improvement, outfit of clothes, piece of furniture or a luxury item.

Matters relating to redundancy and redundancy payments are covered by a booklet published by the Department of Employment entitled *The Redundancy Payments Scheme*, but briefly the amount of redundancy money you receive depends on two things:

1 Your age and the length of 'continuous service' with your employer up to a maximum of twenty years.
2 The amount of your 'normal week's' pay up to a maximum of £100 per week.

Naturally there are rules relating to what constitutes 'continuous service' and 'a normal week's pay', and there are many qualifications as to who is entitled to what and when. Your employer may of course pay you more than the minimum amount he is obliged to pay, by way of a golden handshake in recognition of services to his business, but if he does *not* then it is well worthwhile reading *The Redundancy Payments Scheme* booklet to make sure you have been paid your full redundancy entitlement. The maximum amount of redundancy money which you can receive from the Redundancy Payments Scheme is £3,000 but if your employer is generous, and makes an extra allowance over and above your legal entitlement which does not form part of any contractual agreement, then you may receive up to a total of £10,000 before you pay tax. Payments of less than £10,000 are tax free. The government reimburse your employer with 50 per cent of the legal entitlement to a redundancy payment.

Not everyone is entitled to redundancy payment. For example, you are disqualified from receiving payments in the following circumstances:

a If you have not worked for your employer for more than 104 weeks (two years).
b If you are under the age of 18 and over 65 for a man, and over 60 for a woman.
c If you are a self-employed person in business on your own account, either as an independent contractor, freelance agent, partner in a partnership, or under a contract for services as distinct from a contract of employment.
d If your trade or occupation, eg the Civil Service, a registered dock worker, a share fisherman, or an excluded merchant seaman, has its own scheme.
e If you are a domestic worker in a private household who is a close relative (as defined in the Redundancy Payments Scheme) of the employer.
f If you are dismissed from your job because of inefficiency, unsuitability, or health reasons.
g If you are on a fixed term contract for two years or more, and which was entered into before 6 December 1965.
h If a claim for redundancy payment is not made within six months from the date of termination of employment or referred to an industrial tribunal within a further period of six months.

Retirement

If retirement is a long way away for you, then you may not be too concerned about the effect it will have on your budget, as you obviously cannot put any figures to a situation which is thirty years or even five years ahead. It is impossible to generalise on the financial effects of retirement on your budget, because the permutations of circumstances which might prevail at the time of retirement are endless. Nevertheless it is reasonable to assume that your earnings and expenditure will still be related in the same present day proportions, except for such payments as insurance premiums, ground rent and your mortgage which would remain more or less the same as they are now.

If retirement is imminent, or even if it is not, it is worthwhile thinking about making some provision for retirement having regard to:

a What expenses will you still have at retirement age? Will you still have a mortgage? How many other items will disappear from your present budget? What additional items of expenditure will appear to cover you new found leisure or other pursuits during retirement?
b What will your income be in addition to your State Pension, State Graduated Pension and Supplementary Benefits?
c What extra cash will be forthcoming from the expiration of any insurance policies?

Death

A death in the family will nearly always be unexpected, although the degree of unexpectedness might vary depending on the age and health of the person who dies. Since death is never without cost to someone, it will be necessary to revise your budget to account for:

a Any loss of family income.
b The gain of family income from insurance, government grants, pensions and other similar cash benefits.
c Adjustment of expenditure, ie, omission of certain insurance premiums and any other expenditure not now necessary as a result of a death in a family. For example, settlement of insurance matters could include the paying off of the outstanding mortgage on the home which means there would be no further mortgage payments to account for in your budget.
d Any liabilities for tax.
e The funeral expenses and other costs. The total cost you can expect

depends so much on the choice of many different types of funerals, services, coffins and memorial headstones, that it is impossible to generalise or quote typical costs. It could be as little as £80 and it could be as much as £750 or more. In fact there is so much information on the subject that there is a book entitled *What to do when someone dies* (published by the Consumers Association) which in addition to giving cost guidance, tells you what action should be taken in the event of a death.

Chapter 7

Cutting back on expenditure

The need to economise is more essential in some households than others. For instance, families with a low income need to economise simply to make their money go further, whilst families with a high or comfortable income do not necessarily feel the need to make the same sort of economies, even though sometimes it would do no harm to do so. Whether you belong to a wealthy family or not, there are some economy measures which everyone should try to implement – such as those which conserve energy – in the interest of the nation as a whole, but there is no reason why anyone, wealthy or otherwise, should not try to save themselves money by cutting out unnecessary expenditure. Cutting down is most effective if you attack the big items of expenditure in your budget, but if you can implement a number of small savings, their collective value can be just as effective. Here are a few tips which might help you to make some useful savings – large or small – on your present expenditure.

Anniversaries

There will be some people for whom you will wish to buy special greetings cards, but there will be many others for whom no special card is required. If you bulk buy a quantity of general purpose greetings cards, and especially Christmas greetings cards which are normally on sale very cheaply immediately after Christmas, you will save yourself some money and at the same time equip yourself with a twelve months' stock of greetings cards. Similarly if your children are going through the stage of having and going to lots of birthday parties, it is a good idea to have a stock of suitable gifts and party prizes which you can accumulate at 'sale' times.

Clothing

There is no doubt that households with one or more good dressmakers-cum-knitters in them will save themselves a lot of money, particularly if there are young children in the family. For some unknown reason the cost of clothing for children seems out of all proportion to the cost of clothing for adults, and if you do not have a dressmaker in the family then a sewing machine and a course of instruction in dressmaking is a sound investment. If you can buy clothing to fit 'off the peg' buy only at sale or special offer times; you can anticipate this in your budget by allocating more of your clothing allowance for spending around the winter and summer sale periods, so that you know what you can safely spend. Cleaning bills can also be reduced by purchasing clothing which is washable rather than having to be dry-cleaned; coin-operated dry-cleaning machines in launderettes are much cheaper than regular dry-cleaning services, and adequate for clothes not requiring special pressing.

Decorating

The choice is between doing it yourself or employing a professional decorator to do it for you. There is a theory that if you employ a good decorator you do not need to decorate so often, so if you are not too clever with a paint brush, doing it youself is not necessarily the cheapest way if you have to decorate more frequently. However, the cost of employing a professional decorator need not be prohibitive.

If the houses surrounding yours were built about the same time, then they will need redecorating at about the same time, and if a group of occupiers got together and offered a number of houses to be decorated together this would bring the price down, particularly if some interior decoration is included, as this would mean the decorator could work inside when the weather was not fine enough to decorate externally, and therefore there should be no need to pay an idle time allowance. In this way the job should be over and done with much quicker than doing it yourself, and you avoid the problem of finding ladders, scaffolding and having to buy a tinful of paint when you only need a teaspoonful.

Do-it-yourself

Having work done around the house and garden by builders and gardeners is becoming more and more expensive, due mainly to the high cost of labour. If the only way of getting repairs, maintenance and new work done is to do them yourself, then you will make appreciable cost savings, provided you are skilled enough to make a proper job of the work. The do-it-yourself industry now produces a wide range of materials and tools specially aimed at making life easier for do-it-yourself people. If you have the time to browse around the do-it-yourself stores you will find many time-saving materials and gadgets, and there are now more and more 'hire shops' where you can hire the proper tools, plant, lightweight scaffolding, ladders and power tools to do the job safely and properly. Doing the work safely and properly is very important, so make sure you know and fully understand what you are doing before embarking on any project. Take particular care if you are hoping to improve and enhance the value of your property, as a badly executed extension/alteration can have the reverse effect – even though you may have put a lot of time and money into it.

Electricity

Cutting down on electricity consumption in your home is very much a case of using common sense, by simply switching on your electrical appliances only when it is essential, and switching them off when not required, but cutting down usage of certain appliances can show more savings than others. Therefore, it is essential to be aware of which appliances are expensive to switch on, and which you can afford.

The following information, produced by the Electricity Council, shows the comparison of performance which you can obtain from various electrical appliances for the cost of one unit of electricity (cost per unit will be quoted on your electricity bill).

Living/dining room	
100W light	10 hours' illumination
3kW radiant heater	20 minutes' warmth
Black & white TV	9 hours' viewing
Colour TV	6 hours' viewing
Stereo system	8–10 hours' listening
Hot tray	1½ hours' use
Tape recorder	Over 24 hours' playing
Record player	Over 24 hours' playing
Vacuum cleaner	2–4 hours' use
Bathroom	
Shaver	Over 1,800 shaves
1kW infra-red heater	1 hour's warmth
250W towel rail	4 hours' operation
Kitchen	
Cooker	1 person's daily meals
Kettle	12 pints (6.8 litres) of boiling water
Spin dryer	4 hours' drying
Tumble dryer	½ hour's drying
Refrigerator (compressor type)	1 day's operation
Iron	Over 2 hours' use
Dishwasher	Dinner dishes for a family of four
Food mixer	Over 60 cake mixes
Blender	500 pints (28.4 litres) of soup
Coffee percolator	75 cups of coffee
Extractor fan	15 hours' operation
Waste disposer	1 cwt (50 kilos) of rubbish disposed
Can opener	Over 6,000 cans opened

Cooker hood	10 hours' use
Toaster	70 slices of toast
'On the spot' water heater	Over 3 gallons (13.6 litres) of hot water
2kW fan heater	$\frac{1}{2}$ hour's warmth

Bedroom

Underblanket	Over a week's evening use
Overblanket	Over 2 full night's warmth
2kW convector heater	$\frac{1}{2}$ hour's warmth
Hair rollers	Over 20 hair do's
Hair dryer	3 hours' use
60W reading lamp	Over 16$\frac{1}{2}$ hours' use
Tea maker	35 cups of tea

Garage/workshop

Battery charger	30 hours' charging
100W extension lamp	10 hours' illumination
Power tools	2–4 hours' use

Larger appliances, electric central heating and water heating (all figures approximate and based on average rating of each appliance)–

Food freezer	1$\frac{1}{2}$ units per cubic foot (.028 cubic metre) per week
Automatic washing machine	Weekly wash for family of four 9 units
Twin tub washing machine	Weekly wash for family of four 12 units
Hot water heating	Hot water for family of four (if tank is well lagged) 85 units per week
Shower	A shower a day for a week 5 units
Storage radiators (using lower cost night electricity)	2kW model uses about 2,400 units per heating season (32 weeks), larger ones proportionately more.

Electricaire

Electricaire warm air central heating uses mainly lower cost night rate electricity. Consumption can vary, but average yearly consumption is approximately 1,800 units for every kilowatt rating of the heating system – a 7kW installation for example will use approximately 12,600 units for a 32 week heating season.

Remember: The better insulated the home, the lower the consumption. See *Insulation* on page 77.

Lighting

Look at the lighting in your home. Apart from the obvious suggestion of switching off lights when a room is not in use, you can increase the amount of light by not using strong diffusing shades and save electricity by using low wattage bulbs in places where strong, bright lighting is not required.

Try to use only one room in the evenings and use local lighting, ie table lamps rather than the multi-light chandeliers and wall lights.

Cooking

Use an electric toaster – it is more economical than the cooker grill, and the grill is more economical than the oven for snack meals. Try to avoid having the oven on for cooking only one dish. Organise your cooking so that the oven is fully utilised to cook many dishes, cakes, etc when you have it on. Vegetables will cook quicker if cut smaller; and use a pan which will cook more than one vegetable at a time. Use as little water in the pan as possible without risking it boiling dry, and always cover the pan with a lid; both these cut down on cooking time. If you eat fresh vegetables rather than frozen ones, it is cheaper to cook in a pressure cooker, which will also cook meat more cheaply.

Hot water

Most immersion heaters have alternative temperature settings with thermostatic control for domestic hot water. If you can manage with hot water set at its lowest temperature (and most people should be able to) the thermostat will keep the water at the lower temperature and save you electricity. Not all immersion heaters are fitted with a thermostat (which is a very important device), so check that yours has one fitted; but do not tamper with it yourself without first switching off the electric service at the mains control switch. If you are not sure what to do call in a qualified electrician to check both the temperature setting and thermostat.

The argument as to whether it is cheaper to leave your immersion heater permanently switched on rather than switch it on and off intermittently is by no means proven either way, as so much depends on the quantity of hot water used in the household and the frequency of use. The only way is to try it both ways over three months each way, and see what effect it has on your electricity bill. If you find that switching the immersion heater on and off is cheaper for you, it will be even cheaper if you are well disciplined in remembering to switch it off when not required. You can of course have a time switch installed which will automatically switch the heater on and off at times pre-selected by you, for example it may be the most economical when all members of a household are out for most of the day, to have the hot water programmed so that it comes on for an hour or so in the morning and is then off until the time when everyone gets home in the evening.

You can conserve this hot water by lagging the hot water storage tank and pipework, and by making sure you turn taps off fully and have no dripping taps. Cut down on the amount of hot water used for washing purposes by using less in the basin or bath. Never wash under a running tap, and use cold water for rinsing. A shower unit will use less hot water than a bath.

Do not overfill washing machines and electric kettles. Use only the amount required but always make sure that the heating element is covered. Only use your washing machine when you have full loads and only use electric dryers when you cannot practicably dry by natural means.

Gardening

Growing some of your own food will show considerable saving in your shopping bills but it is just the same as preparing a family budget – to achieve those savings you need to plan well ahead. Planting at the right time of year and planting in staggered time intervals needs to be carefully thought out, so that you do not have a glut of vegetables arriving all at once, or when you are away on holiday, resulting in half the vegetables being wasted or given away – unless of course you can generate some small income by selling your produce to friends and neighbours or through the Women's Institute, or can exchange your surplus for other produce with a neighbour.

You also need garden space available to grow vegetables. If you have a big garden or an allotment, this will not be any problem, but most new houses have relatively small gardens and require detailed attention to produce a layout which will satisfy all of your requirements from the garden in respect of flowerbeds, vegetable patch, greenhouse, garden sheds and leisure use.

There is no point in buying expensive equipment for a small garden or in buying equipment which you use once or twice a year, when so much of this equipment can be hired inexpensively.

There are some excellent books available on the subject of producing food from your garden all year round. Remember that if you have a freezer, surplus produce can be frozen and stored in that.

Heating

Keep your heating appliances at maximum efficiency by having them regularly serviced. Economise as much as you can – but not at the risk of good health – by limiting full heating to one room only, and set the time clocks so that the heat comes on only when you require it on. If you go away from home for a day or longer, re-set the time clock so that it is set on the frost-stat and the heat will come back on again just prior to your return home. On a gas fired heater a one degree reduction on the room thermostat could knock 5 per cent off your heating bill.

Hire-purchase/Budget accounts/Trading cheques/Mail order/Credit cards

This item is included in this chapter because, whilst it will not cut down overall expenditure, it is a means of spreading your financial resources to enable you to buy more of the things you want, sooner. There is nothing wrong with hire-purchase provided you do not overreach yourself. This is where you will find your budget a useful instrument for determining how much you can afford to pay out of your income over a twelve month period, for something you really need. You might otherwise never get round to buying what you want if you wait until you have accumulated sufficient savings to pay cash outright. Even then the price of the goods might have increased at a greater rate than the interest charges would have been on hire-purchase. At least if you commit yourself to a weekly or monthly sum of money for hire-purchase you know that your money is being put to good use and not being frittered away on non-essential spending. Despite recent legislation to protect the purchaser in a hire-purchase transaction, there are still pitfalls to be on your guard against; so make sure you know the true interest rates you are paying and read the small print!

Insulation

Once you have admitted heat into your home and paid for it, it is common sense to try to conserve that heat and keep it in the home as long as possible. So where does the heat eventually escape from your home? According to figures issued by the Department of the Environment:

25 per cent escapes through the roof
35 per cent goes through the wall
10 per cent disappears through the windows
15 per cent is lost through draughts
15 per cent is absorbed into the ground under the floor

These figures are for a typical pre-war semi-detached house without the minimum requirements for modern houses. Heat losses for bungalows and detached houses are in different proportions because the windows, external wall, floor and roof areas are in different proportions.

If you live in a modern house built under the latest Building Regulations certain minimum standards of insulation will already have been provided, but if you live in accommodation which is lacking insulation in any of the places listed above, you should consider the following:

a The more insulation you provide in your roof space the greater will be the reduction of that 25 per cent heat loss through the roof, but the minimum thickness of insulation should be 3″ (75mm).

b Similarly with over one-third of your heat going through the external walls some form of wall insulation must be considered. If you have cavity walls, get several firms to quote you for injecting foam insulation into the walls. There is some risk of dampness appearing after this sort of treatment, so make sure that you select a reputable firm to do the work under guarantee. You must also obtain permission from the Building Surveyor's or Building Inspector's office in your area before having the work done.

c When selecting floor coverings go for a thicker carpet and underlay to reduce heat loss through absorption into the floor. If you have a wooden ground floor with gaps in it and under the skirting board, have it repaired as this is often a cause of heat loss through draughts. If the floor is very bad, covering with hardboard is a fairly inexpensive remedy.

d Eliminate draughts as far as possible by keeping doors closed – a spring-loaded door closing device will help – and make sure that doors and windows fit properly. Draught excluders will also reduce draughts around doors and windows.

e Window insulation, which will reduce loss of heat through the glass in your home, needs the most careful consideration because the cost is not always justified in relation to the heat savings to be made. Invite competitive quotations from a few double-glazing contractors, but before deciding to have the work done consider if the cost of the work is likely to show a substantial reduction in your heating bill – bearing in mind that for an average semi-detached house the heat loss is 10 per cent through the windows – but also that the cost of heating will increase over the years. If you have large areas of glazing in your house the equation of heat saving to cost of double-glazing is more difficult. If you relate your heating bill to the rooms where you use most heat you might find that over 50 per cent of it is used in one or two rooms, and that to double-glaze only the windows in these rooms is a worthwhile money saving exercise. Remember that heat loss is probably greater in the evening when the outside temperature is low, but this can be well insulated against by thick curtaining across the windows, provided of course you do not also cover up the radiators with curtains.

f If you have a disused flue, block it off, but install an air vent somewhere in the flue to avoid condensation.

g If you are building a new house or extension, it is much cheaper to have the insulation provided whilst the building works are being carried out: you can have the cost benefit from the reduction of heat loss much cheaper than by having the extra insulation provided at a later date. You cannot (and indeed should not) eliminate heat loss totally by virtue of the fact that you still need fresh air ventilation in the home. On average the best insulatory measures reduce heat loss by 60 per cent.

Motoring

The cost of running a motor car or cars uses up a large proportion of the sample budget given in this book, and to reduce that expenditure it obviously requires more than just buying petrol from the cheapest garage in town. Look down this check list and see if you can make savings.

1 Use the car less, by walking or cycling.
2 Alternatively, organise group use of the car with friends for going to work, or the station, shopping expeditions, transporting the children to and from school.
3 Is your car too big for the majority of the uses you put it to? Can you manage with a smaller car, having a greater mileage per gallon?
4 Do you need to tear around at top speed wherever you go? This only increases petrol consumption and wear on tyres and brakes.

5 Are you buying the correct grade of petrol? Too low a grade will lead to engine damage eventually, and too high a grade serves no useful purpose at all.
6 Keep the weight in your car down to the minimum, but when you have to carry a heavy load make sure that the weight is evenly distributed.
7 Roof racks should be removed unless you use them frequently as they increase fuel consumption. If you use a roof rack only once or twice a year, hiring one for the odd occasion is cheaper and you do not have any storage problems.

Shopping

Most housewives do not need to be told about buying commodities in season and about the savings to be made by shopping around different supermarkets for the best prices. Similarly, most are aware of the special 'reduced basket' containing bent tins and goods with an imminent sell-by-date. It is also possible to buy many items in a cheaper form or in substitution for something else, but this usually means sacrificing some of the quality – which you may find perfectly acceptable if the savings are great enough. If you have a freezer then you can use this facility to enable you to buy most food items in bulk for storage in the freezer, and to buy and freeze fruit and vegetables in season. Sensible bulk buying will show considerable cost benefits but not only for those with home freezers.

According to the National Consumer Council it is possible to make savings of up to one-third of your housekeeping bill through bulk-buying clubs. These comprise groups of twenty or thirty people organising themselves into shopping clubs, whereby their bulk purchases are divided amongst the club members after they have all contributed their share towards the cost of the purchases. If you would like more details of this, the National Consumer Council (18 Queen Anne's Gate, London, SW1H 9AA) have produced a book called *The Bulk Buy Book* (price £1.00). It gives you the information on how to form a club and also a list of wholesalers where bulk purchases can be made. Unlike shopping in the High Street shopping centre, the price labels in the market place and discount warehouses do not always mean what they say. Somehow the prices in the market and especially the discount warehouses seem to have a margin to haggle over, and if you can acquire the skills of an experienced haggler you will be able to negotiate both large and small price reductions, particularly on furniture, carpets, motor cars and large electrical appliances. You may of course not be offered any guarantees in respect of the goods purchased, or have to put up with poor or non-existent after sales service, but you can guard against this to some extent by buying well-known or branded goods and enquiring about guarantees, after sales service, etc, before you buy.

Local markets often have fruit and vegetables at lower prices than shops, especially those locally produced, and prices may be lower at the end of the day.

Taxation

One way of increasing your income is to pay less tax, not by evasion, but by avoidance. Never take the tax deducted from your earnings as being necessarily correct, simply because it seems difficult for you to check for yourself. This applies particularly to self-employed people who have a greater opportunity to reduce their taxes than employed persons (see Chapter 8) by virtue of being able to charge some expenses, eg part of your private telephone bill, to the business. Make no mistake: it is difficult to keep up with tax legislation even for experts, but good professional advice can soon pay for itself whether you are self-employed or otherwise – more so, if you are paying high taxation.

Telephone

The telephone was invented purely to enable teenage daughters to run up staggering bills for someone else to pay! If you have this problem with children, or anyone else, try buying a simple key operated dialling lock (available from most ironmongers) which will give you some control over the number of outgoing calls without affecting incoming calls. Alternatively, get them to use a system of passing simple code messages which their friends understand, and are expecting, by letting the telephone ring a certain number of times, eg one ring means 'I'm ready to go out', two rings means 'come and pick me up'. On the whole it works successfully – but be prepared for some confusion. There are certain times of the day when you can make telephone calls at a cheaper rate than other times, as follows:

Inland calls

Weekdays	8 am–9 am	Standard rate
	9 am–1 pm	Peak rate
	1 pm–6 pm	Standard rate
	6 pm–8 am	Cheap rate
Weekend	Saturday and Sunday all day cheap rate	

International calls

Weekdays	6 am–8 pm	Standard rate
	All other times	Cheap rate

Obviously you will keep your telephone bill down if you make your calls in the cheaper periods, but also if you limit your calls to those which are essential and cut out those 'inconsequential chat' calls.

Chapter 8

The self-employed person

Being self-employed makes the task of compiling a family budget slightly more difficult. This is not because the items on the budget sheet will necessarily be any different from those on the budget sheets of persons who are not self-employed, but the method of calculating and forecasting income and expenditure will perhaps be different. For instance a self-employed person may use his (the words 'his' or 'he' are used to mean 'her' or 'she' also) home for conducting the whole or part of his business where he deals with paperwork, meets customers, makes and receives business telephone calls, etc. In these circumstances a self-employed person may legitimately be able to charge some of the expenses of running his home to the business accounts, thereby reducing the amounts to be paid from the domestic budget. However, if you do use your own home for conducting the whole or part of your business and you claim tax relief for it, then you may be liable for Capital Gains Tax when eventually you sell your home. Your accountant will advise you best in this respect. For this reason, and also for purposes of tax assessment, it is essential to have a separate set of business accounts and domestic accounts, preferably each with its own bank account. It is not within the scope of this book to deal with business accounts, although it is quite likely, with a small business, that a business cash flow chart will not be dissimilar in layout to the family budget chart, except that the sources of income will be different, as will some of the expenditure.

If, as a self-employed person, your income is regular in both quantity and frequency of receipt, then the method of compiling your family budget will not be very different to that described in the previous chapters of this book, but you will need to exercise greater care in apportioning that part of your income and expenditure which is 'domestic' rather than 'business' budget.

If for any reason your income as a self-employed person (or for that matter as an employee) is irregular either in quantity or frequency or both, then budgeting of any description can be a problem. If this is your situation, then it is advisable at the commencement of your financial year to draw up simultaneously a business cash flow chart (or profit forecast), and a family budget chart, because in both instances there will be essential and vital payments to be made at certain times of the year. This is one way of making sure that you have the cash available to meet those vital payments when they are due. If you are just starting out on your own in business or in any other similar circumstances, where you do not expect to get paid for some time after carrying out your business work, then you will obviously require a cash reserve fund, from which to run both your business and your home during the period between receiving your last wages, salary, grant, or benefit from your previous occupation, up to the time when you actually receive the first income from your new job or business. The amount of money you require in reserve to tide you over these periods obviously depends on the length of the periods when you are without income, so the first requirement is to establish the minimum amount you will need to spend each week or month to keep both the business and your home ticking over.

You can then decide:

(*a*) how many weeks you can survive on your reserve fund before receiving further income, or (*b*) how much you will need in your reserve fund to tide you over the period when you are without income.

You will be able to ascertain this by drawing up a budget chart in a similar manner to *Figure 10*. If you are in difficulty with deficiencies in certain months, and you have no bank overdraft arrangements, then it may be necessary to defer some expenditure until later months when your bank balance on Line 30 looks healthier.

If you find that you have sufficient cash in reserve to tide you over the

		Income [1979]	Jan	Feb	Mar	Apr	May	Jun	Jul	Aug	Sep	Oct	Nov	Dec	Total
Section 1	1	Husband	250				1000	1500		500	500		500	300	4550
	2	Wife	60	60	60	75	60	60	75	60	75	60	60	75	780
	3	Child benefits	48	48	48	60	48	48	60	48	60	48	48	60	624
	4	Other													
	5														
	6	Total income	358	108	108	135	1108	1608	135	608	635	108	608	435	5954
Section 2		Expenditure				5 weeks			5 weeks		5 weeks			5 weeks	
	7	Husband	50	50	50	62	60	60	75	60	75	60	60	75	737
	8	Wife	100	100	100	125	100	100	125	100	125	100	100	125	1300
	9	Mortgage	80	80	80	80	80	80	80	80	80	80	80	80	960
	10	Ground rent and rates	30	30	30	30	30	30	30	30	30	30	30	30	360
	11	Electricity	10	10	10	10	10	10	10	10	10	10	10	10	120
	12	Gas	4	4	4	4	4	4	4	4	4	4	4	4	48
	13	Telephone	7	7	7	7	7	7	7	7	7	7	7	7	84
	14	Heating	11	11	11	11	11	11	11	11	11	11	11	11	132
	15	Insurance	10	10	10	10	10	10	10	10	10	10	10	10	120
	16	Television	10	10	10	10	10	10	10	10	10	10	10	10	120
	17	Clothes	20	20	20	25	20	20	25	20	25	20	20	25	260
	18	Car	10	10	10	10	10	10	10	10	10	10	10	10	120
	19	Anniversaries	10		5		10		5	10	5				45
	20	Christmas and holidays		40		20				520				100	680
	21	House and garden maintenance					30			30				30	90
	22	Furnishings	10	10	10	10	10	10	10	10	10	10	10	10	120
	23	Sports club	5	5	5	5	5	5	5	5	5	5	5	5	60
	24	Childrens' sports/ hobbies	5	5	5	5	5	5	5	5	5	5	5	5	60
	25	Season ticket	10	10	10	10	10	10	10	10	10	10	10	10	120
	26	Sundries	8	8	8	8	8	8	8	8	8	8	8	8	96
	27	Total expenditure	390	420	385	442	430	390	440	950	440	390	390	565	5632
Section 3	28	Cumulative Income	358	466	574	709	1817	3425	3560	4168	4803	4911	5519	5954	
	29	Cumulative expenditure	390	810	1195	1637	2067	2457	2897	3847	4287	4677	5067	5632	
	30	Bank Balance Opening Fig £600	568	256	21	328	350	1568	1263	921	1116	834	1052	922	
	31	Statement													

Figure 10 The self-employed person

period of not receiving income, then there is no problem, other than ensuring that your cash reserve is conserved to last you throughout the period. If, however, you do not have sufficient cash in your business or reserve fund to tide you over the period when you are without income, then you will need to make extra cash available by one of the methods described in Chapter 5. If you cannot borrow money against any of your tangible assets, then you may have to consider borrowing money against anticipated profits to be earned from your business, or from a special project which you are hoping to embark upon.

Borrowing money in this way is sometimes very difficult, depending on how well the money lender knows you and/or your business and on the degree of risk of failure/success which the money lender attaches to your proposals. You may well find yourself not only having to pay interest charges over the odds, but also giving away a share of the equity from the project to the money lender. However, this would be strictly for the business accounts side and perhaps requiring professional advice, but nevertheless having an influence on the domestic budget.

A self-employed person's family budget with irregular income may well look something like *Figure 10*. It works in exactly the same way as the budget discussed in earlier chapters but there are a few points in addition, which self-employed people should take note of.

Line 1 – Husband's income

1	Husband	250				1000	1500		500	500		500	300	4550

The husband's income is forecasted as being received at different times, and in different amounts related to completion of certain business transactions, which could be in stages or in their entirety, depending on the arrangements made with customers for payments on account, etc. Note also that as with the family budget for an employee, the income shown is after deduction of tax, National Insurance contributions and any other business outgoing. Therefore, in order to arrive at the net amount of income the business accounts side would have to make deductions for those outgoings.

Self-employed people do not PAYE – as do employees – they pay 'Schedule D tax assessment' instead, which is based on the profits earned by the business and is paid normally twice per annum (1 January and 1 July). A separate set of business accounts must be kept in order to ensure that you are taxed fairly by the Inland Revenue. Note also that if your business has a turnover in excess of £10,000 per annum you will be liable to pay VAT. Different rules for National Insurance contributions also apply to self-employed people and you should therefore ensure that you are fully aware of your liability for both tax and National Insurance contributions in advance of spending all of your income.

It may be advisable for you to have not only a monthly check on your family budget, but also a monthly audit on your business accounts in order that you have some idea of the profitability (or otherwise) of your business. You will then have some idea of how much of your earnings will need to be held in reserve to meet your tax liability at the end of each six month tax period.

Line 2 – The wife's income

2	Wife	60	60	60	75	60	60	75	60	75	60	60	75	780

This could be her earnings from a job not connected with her husband's business, but it could also be her income as a partner in her husband's business. There are certain tax benefits to be gained on the business accounts side by taking the wife as a paid partner in the business, but your accountant will advise on this matter.

Line 3 – Child Benefits

3	Child benefits	48	48	48	60	48	48	60	48	60	48	48	60	624

The children of 'self-employed people' entitle their parents to the same benefits as 'employees', and the same rules apply to both sample budgets.

Lines 7 and 8 – Husband's and wife's allowance

7	Husband	50	50	50	62	60	60	75	60	75	60	60	75	737
8	Wife	100	100	100	125	100	100	125	100	125	100	100	125	1300

The allowances on these two lines are intended to cover the same items discussed on page 21. A self-employed person may well find, however, that these expenses are rather high in comparison due to entertaining customers and potential clients, hotel bills, etc. Some of this expenditure will be accounted for in the 'business accounts' so be careful how you allocate this expenditure in your 'family budget'.

Lines 9 to 14 inclusive

9	Mortgage	80	80	80	80	80	80	80	80	80	80	80	80	960
10	Ground rent and rates	30	30	30	30	30	30	30	30	30	30	30	30	360
11	Electricity	10	10	10	10	10	10	10	10	10	10	10	10	120
12	Gas	4	4	4	4	4	4	4	4	4	4	4	4	48
13	Telephone	7	7	7	7	7	7	7	7	7	7	7	7	84
14	Heating	11	11	11	11	11	11	11	11	11	11	11	11	132

Remember we are dealing with a self-employed person whose income is irregular in both quantity and frequency of receipt. If these are your circumstances it will almost certainly be necessary for you to pay as many of your expenses as you can on a weekly or monthly basis, so that you avoid having to pay out large sums of money at an awkward time, in both your business and domestic budgets. Such things as mortgages/rent, rates, electricity, gas, telephones, car insurance, season ticket, licences and club subscriptions can be arranged to be paid on a monthly basis either direct to the recipients or through your bank. Most banks offer a service whereby you open a separate account for paying out money to a selected list of individuals or companies. You pay a fixed sum into this account every month and the bank will allow you to pay the full amount of each bill from the list at any time of the year.

It would work something like this. Make a list of the annual payments you would like to pay on a monthly basis, say,

	£
Rates	360
Gas	48
Electricity	120
Telephone	84
Ground rent	50
Car insurance	100
Other insurance	20
TV licence	21
Season ticket	120
Subscriptions	107
Car tax	50
	1,080

∴ monthly amount to be paid into bank

$$= \frac{1{,}080}{12} = £90.00$$

You can pay any of the amounts from the above list, in full, at any time you wish (provided you have not defaulted on your monthly payments into the bank). This means that you can make some discount savings on certain things for paying in advance (eg buying a season ticket) or by paying your car tax annually instead of tri-annually. The bank may not provide this service free of charge, and they will also charge you normal overdraft interest when your budget payment account is overdrawn, but this would not prevent you from continuing to pay out money to those individuals or companies on the 'selected list'. Obviously any shortfall between the amount of money paid in and money paid out at the end of the financial year will have to be made good, but if you carry out your budgeting properly throughout the year, you will be aware of any shortfall to be made up long before the end of the year.

Line 15 – Insurance

15	Insurance	10	10	10	10	10	10	10	10	10	10	10	10	120

It may be possible and advantageous to secure more favourable terms for your family's personal and property insurance, by grouping it with the insurances associated with your business. If you run the business entirely by yourself and there is no one to take your place in the event of your illness, then it is advisable that you protect yourself adequately with an insurance policy which will provide you with an income during your illness. You may also be able to get speedier treatment for an illness by being a private patient under a BUPA or similar type of scheme, thereby minimising the amount of time you are away from your business.

Line 18 – Car

18	Car	10	10	10	10	10	10	10	10	10	10	10	10	120

In *Figure 10* the costs of providing and running the car are accounted for entirely in the business accounts, and the only cost in the family budget is to provide petrol for private mileage.

The remaining items on the *Figure 10* budget are the same as the budget on page 38, including the arithmetic in SECTION 3 of the chart, except that you will see on Line 30 in the months of March and April our self-employed person has gone into the red (grey column) by virtue of the cumulative expenditure on Line 29 exceeding the cumulative income on Line 28.

Fortunately the bank manager has been satisfied that the income shown due in the month of May is very likely to be received, and has agreed to allow the account to be overdrawn to the extent shown, on the strength of the anticipated payment into the bank. If your self-employed person had been unable to satisfy the bank manager that the income he was expecting would be received in due course, then it would have been necessary to make other arrangements (selling an asset or borrowing) to raise the extra money, to tide the home and business over the two difficult months.

Chapter 9

And finally – have a go at your budget

You will find your budget a useful tool in manipulating your money, not just at the commencement of your budget, but throughout the entire period. For instance, if you had budgeted to buy a new television set say in September at a cost of £300.00, and you saw the same television in a sale in July at £200.00 but could not strictly afford to buy it then, you could take your budget to your bank manager, explain this to him, and he might well, in these circumstances, permit an overdraft between July and September, to enable you to take advantage of the bargain television offer.

Similarly, a holiday in peak periods will cost more than an out-of-season holiday, but you may not have the money available at the right time to take the cheaper holiday. If you can show your bank manager that to save yourself money you will need a small overdraft for a short period, then he might be sympathetic, but only if you can present him with a sensible budget which he can see, by looking at Lines 30 and 31, is working properly for you.

You will find a variety of uses to which your budget can be put and you might even enjoy filling in your actual monthly income and expenditure just to see how accurate your forecasting was. So why not have a go at preparing a budget for your family on the sheets provided opposite and over the page?

		Income [1979]	Jan	Feb	Mar	Apr	May	Jun	Jul	Aug	Sep	Oct	Nov	Dec	Total
Section 1	1	Husband													
	2	Wife													
	3	Child benefits													
	4	Other													
	5														
	6	Total income													
Section 2		Expenditure													
	7	Husband													
	8	Wife													
	9	Mortgage													
	10	Ground rent and rates													
	11	Electricity													
	12	Gas													
	13	Telephone													
	14	Heating													
	15	Insurance													
	16	Television													
	17	Clothes													
	18	Car													
	19	Anniversaries													
	20	Christmas and holidays													
	21	House and garden maintenance													
	22	Furnishings													
	23	Sports club													
	24	Childrens' sports/ hobbies													
	25	Freezer stocks													
	26	Sundries													
	27	Total expenditure													
Section 3	28														
	29														
	30														
	31														

Summary of monthly expenditure Year

Line	7	8	9	10	11	12	13	14	15	16	17	17	17	18	18	18	19	20	21	22	23	24	25	26	
											Clothing			Car											
Item / Date	Husband	Wife	Mortgage	Rates	Electricity	Gas	Phone	Heating	Insurance	Television	Husbnd	Wife	Childn	Petrol	Tax & insrnce	Serv & repairs	Annivs	Christmas Holidays	House & garden	Furnishings	Sports club	Childrens' hobbies	Freezer	Sundries	Remarks

Check list of items for your family budget

Accident
Adoption
Air conditioning
Alimony
Allotment
Anniversaries
Anti-freeze
Antiques
Apartment
Apprenticeship
Aquaria
Attic extension

Baby
Baby sitter
Bicycle
Birthdays
Books
Boy Scouts
Burglar alarm

Camping
Car
Caravan
Cassette tapes
Chauffeur
Chiropodist
Christmas
Church
Cinema
Clothes
Club
Coins

Daily help
Dancing
Death
Decorations
Dentist
Depreciation
Divorce
Doctor
Do-it-yourself
Donations
Double-glazing
Dry cleaning

Education
Electricity
Entertainment

Fares
Fees –
  Accountant
  Agent
  Architect
  College
  Consultant
  Driving school
  Exam
  Membership
  School
  Solicitor
  Surveyor
Fencing
Flowers
Flying
Freezer
Funeral
Furniture

Gambling
Garage
Garden
Gardener
Gas
Girl Guides
Ground rent

Hairdressing
Health
Health Club
Heating
Hire Purchase

Hobbies
Holidays
Home –
  Buying
  Extension
  Improvements
Hospital

Illness
Insulation
Insurance

Jewellery

Kennels
Knitting

Laundry
Lessons
Licence –
  Dog
  Driving
  Gun
  Radio
  Television
Loans

Magazines
Maintenance
Marriage

Medicine
Mortgage
Motor cycle
Music

Newspapers
Nursery

Oil
Optician

Painting
Parties
Passport
Petrol
Pets
Philately
Photography
Playgroup
Pocket money
Presents

Rates
Records
Redundancy
Removals
Rents
Repairs
Retirement
Road Tax

Season ticket
Sewing
Shares
Smoking
Solid fuel
Sport
Stamp Duty
Storage

Taxation
Telephone
Television
Theatre
Tools
Travel

Uniform
Union subscription
University

Vet

Wedding
Will
Wine
Wine making

Youth Club